The Science of Jealousy

CRAFTED BY SKRIUWER

Copyright © 2024 by Skriuwer.

All rights reserved. No part of this book may be used or reproduced in any form whatsoever without written permission except in the case of brief quotations in critical articles or reviews.

For more information, contact : **kontakt@skriuwer.com** (www.skriuwer.com)

TABLE OF CONTENTS

CHAPTER 1: UNDERSTANDING JEALOUSY—WHAT IT IS

- Definition and key differences from envy
- Common physical and emotional signs
- Reasons jealousy arises in various relationships
- Why recognizing early signs can help prevent bigger problems

CHAPTER 2: THE EVOLUTION OF JEALOUSY

- Ancient survival functions of jealousy
- Jealousy in small tribes and early human groups
- Shifts in modern society's view of jealousy
- Why this emotion remains powerful today

CHAPTER 3: HOW THE BRAIN SHAPES JEALOUSY

- Key brain areas involved in jealousy
- Link between fear response and jealous thoughts
- Role of chemicals and hormones in fueling suspicion
- Ways to use this knowledge for calmer reactions

CHAPTER 4: KINDS OF JEALOUSY

- Romantic jealousy vs. friendship jealousy
- Sibling rivalry and family jealousy
- Achievement-based or workplace jealousy
- Unique triggers in different life areas

CHAPTER 5: SOCIAL FACTORS IN JEALOUSY

- Cultural norms that raise or lower jealous feelings
- Group and peer influences on competitiveness
- Media and social media effects on comparisons
- Why understanding social triggers matters

CHAPTER 6: JEALOUSY IN EARLY YEARS

- How children first show jealous behavior
- Common reasons: sharing toys or parental attention
- Teaching kids healthy emotional coping
- Long-term impact of childhood jealousy

CHAPTER 7: JEALOUSY IN ROMANCE

- Why romantic jealousy feels so intense
- Signs of unhealthy vs. mild jealousy
- Communication tips for partners facing fear of loss
- Balancing trust and personal boundaries

CHAPTER 8: JEALOUSY IN FAMILIES

- Common family-based jealousies—parental approval, siblings
- Tension in extended families or step-families
- Acknowledging each member's needs fairly
- Ways to keep family bonds strong

CHAPTER 9: JEALOUSY IN DIFFERENT CULTURES

- Varying expressions of jealousy around the world
- How traditions and customs shape jealous behavior
- Impact of global blending of cultural norms
- Lessons from cross-cultural insights

CHAPTER 10: JEALOUSY IN ANIMALS

- Signs of jealousy in pets and other species
- Possible evolutionary advantages of guarding resources
- Studies on social animals' jealous behaviors
- What this reveals about our own emotions

CHAPTER 11: RECOGNIZING JEALOUSY

- Bodily signals and mental clues
- Common thinking patterns that hint at jealousy
- Spotting hidden jealousy in others
- Turning early awareness into constructive action

CHAPTER 12: JEALOUSY AT SCHOOL

- Classroom competition and social comparisons
- Friendship changes and exclusion
- Tackling jealousy in group projects or sports
- Helping students channel envy into motivation

CHAPTER 13: JEALOUSY AT WORK

- Why workplaces can spark envy—promotions, pay
- Identifying jealousy in coworkers or bosses
- Strategies for fair recognition and open teamwork
- Staying calm when workplace tensions rise

CHAPTER 14: EFFECTS OF JEALOUSY ON EMOTIONS

- How jealousy links to anxiety, anger, or sadness
- Physical toll of chronic jealous thoughts
- Long-term impact on self-esteem and relationships
- Finding balance when feeling threatened

CHAPTER 15: WAYS TO HANDLE JEALOUSY

- Calming techniques and practical exercises
- Open communication tips without blame
- Challenges of supporting someone else's insecurity
- Building positive personal habits to reduce envy

CHAPTER 16: HEALTHY BONDS WITHOUT JEALOUSY

- *Trust and respect as protective factors*
- *Setting boundaries in families and friendships*
- *Recognizing normal vs. harmful jealousy*
- *Encouraging openness and shared understanding*

CHAPTER 17: HELPING OTHERS FACE JEALOUSY

- *Identifying clues when a friend or relative is jealous*
- *Approaching gently and listening carefully*
- *Balancing kindness with personal limits*
- *Offering support without fueling dependence*

CHAPTER 18: JEALOUSY IN HISTORY

- *Ancient myths revealing jealousy's destructive potential*
- *Court intrigues and royal jealousy in past eras*
- *Historical conflicts driven by envy*
- *Lessons from how societies managed or mismanaged jealousy*

CHAPTER 19: WRONG IDEAS ABOUT JEALOUSY

- *Myths about jealousy's role in love and life*
- *Common stereotypes—gender, guilt, insecurity*
- *Why these misunderstandings hinder real solutions*
- *Correcting false beliefs for healthier perspectives*

CHAPTER 20: WHAT MIGHT HAPPEN NEXT WITH JEALOUSY

- *Future trends in social life and technology*
- *Possible new triggers, from AI to shifting relationship norms*
- *Optimistic outlooks—better tools for managing emotions*
- *How adapting together can keep jealousy from ruling us*

Chapter 1: Understanding Jealousy: What It Is

Jealousy is a feeling that many people experience. It can feel like worry, fear, or anger when we think someone else has taken something that we care about. Sometimes we might feel it when we see someone getting attention we want for ourselves. Other times, we might feel it if we believe someone else is getting more praise or love than we are. It can come from a wish to hold on to something we value. This strong emotion can cause uneasy thoughts in our minds and unpleasant sensations in our bodies.

When we talk about jealousy, we should think about what it is and what it is not. Some people mix up the words "envy" and "jealousy," but they do not mean the same thing. Envy usually means wishing to have something that another person has, such as a new toy or a special talent. Jealousy, on the other hand, focuses on not wanting someone else to take or share something that we think belongs to us, like love, attention, or an important spot in someone's life.

There are times in life when jealousy might happen in small ways. For example, if you see your friend chatting happily with a new classmate, you might feel worried that your friend will not pay attention to you anymore. In that moment, you might feel a tingle in your stomach, or perhaps a tight feeling in your chest. You might start to imagine your friend hanging out with the new classmate instead of with you. These thoughts can make you upset, and you might try to protect your friendship in different ways. You might rush over to your friend to remind them that you are still around. Or you might act out in a way to get your friend's attention back.

Jealousy is a tricky emotion, because it can bring out many other feelings. It can lead to anger if you feel you are losing something important and there is nothing you can do about it. It can lead to sadness if you think you are not special to the person you care about. It might also lead to shame if you feel guilty for not trusting the person you love. On top of that, you might feel embarrassed for having these thoughts at all. These different feelings can show up all at once, making jealousy a complicated experience.

People can feel jealousy in many parts of their lives. It can appear in friendships, romance, or even in families. Brothers and sisters might feel jealous when a parent seems to give more attention to one child than another. This is a common reason for sibling arguments. In school, a student might feel jealous if a classmate gets more kind words from the teacher. In relationships, a person might feel jealous if they think their partner is spending time with someone else in a way that feels threatening. These situations show how widespread jealousy can be.

The feeling of jealousy often shows up with certain physical signs. You might notice your heart beating faster or your hands getting sweaty. Sometimes people feel warm or flushed in the face. Others might feel a knot in their stomach or their chest. These body reactions come from the stress and worry linked to jealousy. The body goes on high alert, worried that something precious might be taken away.

At times, jealousy can be seen as a signal that something important might be at risk. It is not always a bad thing to notice this feeling. If we pay attention to it, we might see that it points to a concern or an unmet need. For example, if you feel jealous because your best friend is spending a lot of time with someone else, it might mean you are craving more time with them, or that you fear losing your place in their life. Recognizing this can help you talk calmly with your friend, share your worries, and ask for reassurance. This can bring you closer and help both of you understand each other.

However, jealousy can become hurtful if it grows too big or happens too often. If you feel jealous too easily, you might stress your relationships. You might become clingy, or you might start accusing friends or loved ones without real proof. This can push them away, leaving you feeling even more insecure. Sometimes, jealousy might lead to controlling actions, like telling someone whom they can or cannot talk to. This can cause a lot of pain in a relationship. It can also harm your sense of self-worth, because you might feel that you are not enough on your own.

Jealousy does not come from nowhere. Each person has a story and a set of experiences that shape how they react to certain situations. Some people might feel more suspicious or afraid because they have been hurt before. Others might have low self-esteem, which can cause them to be more easily jealous. Past experiences, like losing a close friend or going through a breakup, can make a person more watchful. This emotional habit can make it harder to stay calm when new moments of fear come up.

Jealousy might also connect to our sense of belonging. We often want to be valued by others. We want to know that we matter. When we think someone else is taking our spot, we might fear that we will be left out. This longing to be included or favored sometimes causes people to keep a close watch on what others do. For example, a child might become upset if they feel a teacher is smiling more at another student. This might seem like a small thing, but to the child, it can feel huge because it touches that deep wish to be liked.

There is no single cause of jealousy. It can come from many directions, like our past, our personal traits, and our current worries. It can show up quickly, almost without warning, and it can change how we see a situation. Suddenly, we may interpret a simple smile between two people as a sign that we are losing something. Once jealousy appears, it can be tough to see the truth of what is actually happening, because our fears may take over.

An important point in understanding jealousy is to recognize that it is often rooted in fear. It is a fear that someone might replace us, ignore us, or take away something we love. When you pull back the layers of this emotion, you will often find worry about not being good enough, or about not being chosen. Jealousy can highlight areas in our lives where we feel insecure. At the same time, it can draw our attention to areas that we value dearly, such as love or respect.

Because jealousy can be so intense, it often plays a big part in stories and myths all over the world. In many tales, jealousy drives characters to do extreme things. For instance, in some old legends, a person becomes so jealous that they try to trick or hurt another. While these are just stories, they show us that jealousy has been a part of the human experience for a very long time. People have tried to make sense of this feeling by telling tales of its power and the consequences it can bring.

Sometimes, jealousy can hide behind other words. A person might not say, "I am jealous." They might say they are just concerned or that they feel suspicious. This is because jealousy can feel shameful. It can make us feel small or embarrassed, as though we cannot trust those we love or trust ourselves. Admitting to jealousy takes honesty and courage. Yet, talking about it can help us see the real problem behind the feeling. Maybe we need to talk about our fears. Maybe we just need a bit of reassurance. When we speak openly, we can stop jealousy from growing in silence.

It is also key to notice that jealousy is not always based on facts. Sometimes, it comes from the thoughts in our own heads, which might not reflect reality. We might misread a situation or assume the worst. Once that seed of doubt is planted in our mind, it can be hard to see things clearly. We might seek "proof" that someone is about to wrong us, and in doing so, we interpret harmless actions in a negative light. This can cause a snowball effect, leading to bigger and bigger misunderstandings.

Understanding jealousy does not mean judging it as all good or all bad. It is a normal emotion that most people feel at some point. Some experts say that a small amount of jealousy can sometimes remind us that we care about a relationship. It can push us to stay connected and to show our appreciation for the people in our lives. But if it grows too large, it can cause harm, making us anxious or controlling. It is important to learn to spot it before it becomes unmanageable.

In day-to-day life, people handle jealousy in different ways. Some try to hide it, pretending it is not there. Others express it right away through anger or tears. Others might try to distract themselves. The way each person reacts to jealousy can depend on their personality, their past experiences, and how they learned to handle strong feelings. In some families, people might talk freely about emotions. In others, people might keep feelings inside. When jealousy is not acknowledged, it can build up over time and turn into resentment.

Understanding jealousy as a child or teen can be tough, because it might be the first time you have felt this powerful swirl of feelings. You might not know what to call it at first. You might only know that you feel uncomfortable when you see your friend play with someone else. Or you might feel uneasy when you see a parent hugging your sibling more than you. As you grow older, you begin to notice that your thoughts and worries can make the feelings stronger or weaker. Learning about jealousy can help you name what is happening, which can lead to healthier ways to respond.

Some people associate jealousy with relationships between adults, but it can start early in life. Even very young children can show signs of jealousy if they see a parent picking up another child or giving more attention to a sibling. This can appear in small things, like a child acting fussy when the new baby is held by their mother. This is a common and natural reaction. Kids do not want to lose the comfort and care they have come to expect. While these feelings can be intense, grown-ups can help kids by showing them that they are still loved.

To truly understand jealousy, we should recognize that it can be a mix of protective feelings, fears, and hopes. It tries to shield something important from being lost. The mind tries to warn us of possible threats, and the body reacts to this warning. It is a sign of the value we place on the people and things we love. Without that care, we might not feel worried at all. Yet, we have to be careful about letting jealousy grow so large that it pushes us to act in unkind or unfair ways.

Jealousy can be shaped by the world around us, too. For instance, certain ideas or stories in movies might suggest that if a person you love talks to someone else, you should feel suspicious. These messages can shape how we react. We might think it is normal to feel jealous in every situation like that. But real life is more nuanced. Not every conversation or friendship is a threat to a relationship. It takes patience to learn the difference and to trust that the people we care about also care about us.

Even though jealousy can be very unpleasant, understanding it is the first step to handling it in a helpful way. When we notice we are jealous, we can pause and think about why this is happening. We can ask ourselves, "Do I feel like I am not good enough?" or "What am I afraid of losing?" This can help us find the real reason for our jealousy. Once we see the reason, we can then talk about it or think about it calmly. Over time, this can ease the worries that feed jealousy.

In some situations, it might also help to reflect on our sense of self-worth. If we feel sure of our own value, we might not be as easily shaken by someone else's success or by the fear of losing something. When our self-esteem is low, we might look for proof that we are going to be left out or replaced. By growing a stronger belief in our own abilities and worth, we can lower the chances of jealousy taking over.

While jealousy is something we might see as purely negative, it can be a signal that we need to address a concern. If handled in a caring way, it can lead to better understanding of ourselves and others. However, when jealousy is left unchecked, it can damage trust and personal well-being. Recognizing jealousy as part of normal human emotions helps us see that we are not alone in feeling it.

Many people have dealt with it in the past, and many people will deal with it in the future.

Jealousy is an old emotion, shaped by our hopes, fears, and experiences. At its root, it reminds us that we have things and people that are precious to us. Learning to see it clearly can help us avoid the traps it sets, such as misreading a situation or jumping to conclusions. If we learn to pause, ask ourselves questions, and talk with honesty, we can keep jealousy from becoming too big.

In this book, we will look at jealousy from many angles. We will see where it comes from and how it can appear in different parts of life. We will also see how it can shape the way we think and act. By the end, we will have a deeper understanding of jealousy and how we can handle it with care. The more we know, the better we can face it in a way that helps, rather than hurts, our relationships and our own sense of self.

Chapter 2: The Evolution of Jealousy: Past and Present

Jealousy did not just appear out of the blue. It has roots that go far back in human history. To understand why we feel jealous, it helps to think about how humans have lived and grown over time. Long ago, people lived in small groups, hunting and gathering food. In these groups, certain behaviors were important for survival. If someone felt that their place in the group was threatened, they might react strongly. This was because belonging to a group was a matter of life and death. Being pushed out could mean less protection from danger.

Early humans had to work together to find food and stay safe from wild animals. Sharing and cooperation were important, but at the same time, people also had to watch out for their own needs. If someone thought that another person was taking something that belonged to them, they might react with aggression or caution. These actions were part of an instinct to protect what was theirs. Over thousands of years, people might have become more alert to signs of losing what they valued. Some researchers suggest that jealousy grew out of this need to protect one's mate, family, or belongings. It could be a signal to act before it was too late.

When we think about the past, we can see how jealousy could keep people on guard. For instance, if a person thought their partner was giving attention to someone else, it could mean that they might lose support in raising children. Long ago, if one parent left, the other might find it harder to get enough food or protect the children. The feeling of jealousy could push a person to act in ways that stopped this from happening, like guarding the relationship or confronting a possible rival. While these actions might be harmful in some ways, they might have helped some families survive in a challenging world.

In old stories and records, there are many mentions of jealousy. For example, ancient myths often describe gods and goddesses acting out of jealousy when they see mortals or other gods getting more attention or devotion. These stories mirror the human fear of losing something important. Even in early laws and traditions, we see rules about loyalty, marriage, and property that might have formed partly because of jealousy. People have long recognized that jealousy can lead to fights or betrayal, so they tried to place rules to keep things stable.

As human groups grew larger and formed villages, then towns, and finally cities, people had to live together in more complex ways. They had different roles in society, such as leaders, workers, and traders. New kinds of relationships formed, and with them came new reasons for jealousy. A person might envy someone who rose to a higher position, or feel jealous if they thought their spouse was not faithful. These feelings often appeared in records and letters, showing that jealousy was part of daily life.

Over time, ideas about jealousy also evolved. People started to write about it, trying to explain why it happens and how to handle it. In some places, jealousy was seen as a sign of strong love, especially in romantic relationships. In other times, people warned that jealousy was a dangerous feeling that could lead to anger and harm. Philosophers wrote about it, religious texts gave lessons on how to resist it, and poets composed verses about the pain of jealousy. This mix of views shows that people have always struggled to find the right balance between caring for someone and fearing their loss.

In many early cultures, marriage was seen as a way to form alliances between families or tribes. Jealousy could come up if someone felt that another person was breaking these alliances. In some societies, strict rules were set about how men and women should act to reduce the chance of jealousy. These rules might have limited people's choices, but they also aimed to keep peace. Over time, as societies changed, people began to value personal love and choice in relationships more. This opened the door to different expressions of jealousy, since people could pick partners based on affection rather than just family agreements.

Jealousy is not unique to one part of the world. You can find stories and records of it in ancient civilizations across every continent. It took different shapes based on local traditions, but the feeling was similar: a fear of losing what one held dear. This can be seen in old artwork, where scenes might show rivals competing for the affection of a ruler, or a person scowling while watching someone else receive praise. These expressions remind us that jealousy is not new.

As we reach modern times, jealousy continues to be a part of human life. However, the ways it appears might be different because of changes in culture and technology. Today, people can see many others on social media, which can spark jealousy if we believe someone else's life looks better than ours. For instance, you might see pictures of a friend with new friends, and you might worry that you are left out. Or you might see a partner liking someone else's photos, and feel jealous about what that means. While the feeling is old, the situations can be quite modern.

When looking at jealousy over time, we notice that it often has two main parts: the concern about losing what we value and the wish to keep or protect it. In the past, this could mean defending a small community or a loved one who provided help in daily survival. In the present, it might mean sending a text to a friend to make sure they still care about you. The forms have changed, but the core feeling remains.

Scientists studying the evolution of emotions have looked at jealousy to see if it has a purpose. They point out that if jealousy makes a person act to guard a relationship or a resource, it can be a benefit in some ways, since it might stop a person from neglecting important connections. But if it becomes too strong, it can lead to damaging or violent behavior, which is harmful to both the jealous person and those around them. In this sense, jealousy might be helpful in small amounts but risky in large doses.

Modern society has tried to understand jealousy through psychology, sociology, and other fields of study. Psychologists look at how thoughts and feelings lead to jealous behavior, while sociologists notice how social rules affect when and why people feel jealous. For example, some cultures might expect people to be more open with their relationships, leading to fewer jealous feelings. Others might encourage close bonds and stricter rules around loyalty, which might increase the chance of jealous thoughts.

At the same time, as we have gained knowledge about the brain, we see that certain areas in our heads light up when we think someone is threatening what we value. Our brain's alarm system might start working, making us feel anxious or stressed. We might replay images in our mind of the person we love with someone else, or we might imagine our friends laughing and having fun without us. These mental pictures can make the jealous feeling grow.

Society has also changed the way we talk about jealousy. In some periods, jealousy was seen almost as an honor, as if it meant you cared strongly about a partner. Some cultures might have viewed it as proof that you really valued someone. In other times, jealousy was criticized, and people were told it was a weakness or a sin. Today, there might be a mix of these views, with some seeing jealousy as normal and others viewing it as something to watch out for.

The presence of jealousy in stories, movies, and popular music shows that it remains a topic people find interesting. Many plots revolve around the worry that a person's loved one might leave them or that a rival might replace them. This has been a theme in dramatic tales, from ancient plays to modern television. It captures our attention because we recognize the strong feelings inside the characters. They speak to a common emotion many of us have felt at some point in our lives.

Some experts believe that part of the reason jealousy has lasted so long is its link to bonding. If we worry that someone is going to take our place, it might motivate us to act kinder or to show more appreciation to those we love. This does not always happen, but it can. Jealousy might spur us to not take our bonds for granted. Still, we must remember that this emotion can also break bonds if it is handled poorly.

In recent times, we also see how jealousy can be triggered by social media. We can see hundreds of pictures of people we know, along with their happy moments, successes, or new relationships. This steady stream of images can make us feel like we are missing out. It can also spark jealousy if we see someone getting attention or kindness from people we care about. Some people find themselves checking what their friends or partners are doing online, searching for signs of potential threats. This can feed into unhealthy habits.

Yet, not everyone experiences jealousy in the same way. Some people are more likely to feel it, either because of their personality or their past experiences. Others might have been taught to trust more or to talk about their worries before they grow. Cultural background can also make a difference. In certain places, open talk about feelings is encouraged, while in other places, people might hide or deny these feelings. Understanding these differences can help us see how jealousy evolves in each individual.

While the emotion of jealousy has been around for ages, our ways of dealing with it can evolve. If we grow in how we talk about our fears, if we learn more about our own worth, and if we set healthy boundaries in our relationships, we can lessen the damage jealousy can cause. We do not have to be stuck with the same patterns from our ancient past. We can learn better habits that allow us to handle jealousy in ways that are kinder to ourselves and others.

When we compare the past and the present, we see a few key points. First, jealousy has always been tied to the fear of losing something or someone special. Second, the ways people have shown and managed jealousy have changed as social structures, beliefs, and relationships have changed. Third, our modern lives give us new triggers for jealousy, but they also offer new ways to handle it, such as therapy, open conversations, and safe places to share feelings.

Looking back at how jealousy formed helps us understand that it is not just a random emotion. It is part of the human story, shaped by survival needs, cultural rules, and personal experiences. It warns us that we might lose something dear, but it also carries risks if it becomes too big. Knowing this can help us feel less alone when jealousy strikes. We realize that countless people before us have faced this same feeling and learned lessons about how to cope with it.

As we continue to talk about jealousy in this book, we will keep these roots in mind. Seeing the bigger picture helps us handle our own jealous feelings more calmly. We can remind ourselves that jealousy is a normal part of human life, dating back to ancient times when protecting what we had was important for survival. We can also remember that we have more tools now than our ancestors did. We can reach out for help, talk about our fears, and find healthier ways to manage this powerful emotion.

In closing, jealousy has existed in our species for a very long time. It has shaped stories, laws, art, and ways of living. It can be found in the old myths of many lands and in the everyday moments of our modern world. By looking at where jealousy came from and how it has changed, we gain insight into why it still appears in our lives today. We can accept it as part of our shared human history, and we can learn to face it with kindness and understanding, both for ourselves and for those around us.

Chapter 3: How the Brain Shapes Jealousy

Jealousy is more than just a feeling in our hearts. It also has roots in the brain. Our brains control how we sense threats, how we react to fear, and how we remember past events. These parts all come together to shape how we feel when we think we might lose something special. By looking at the brain, we can better see why jealousy can feel so strong at times.

The Brain and Emotions

First, let us talk about emotions in general. Emotions like happiness, sadness, or anger often begin in the parts of our brain that handle signals of reward or danger. When something good happens, the reward center might release certain chemicals. When we face danger, other parts of the brain signal the release of hormones that help us decide if we should fight or run away. While jealousy is not exactly the same as fear or anger, it can bring up some of the same responses.

One key player in many emotions is the amygdala. The amygdala is shaped a bit like an almond, and it sits deep inside the brain. It helps us notice and respond to threats. If we see something that makes us feel we are in danger of losing someone or something, the amygdala might become active. It can then work with other parts of the brain to produce signals that we feel as worry, stress, or anger. That is why, when jealousy flares, our hearts might beat faster, and our muscles might tense up.

Another important part of the brain is the hippocampus. The hippocampus helps us store and recall memories. If you have ever felt jealous because you remembered a past event—maybe a friend ignoring you or a partner leaving you out—the hippocampus is involved. It brings back the memory of that situation, which can feed the new jealous feeling. Sometimes, our memories can make jealousy stronger than it needs to be. For example, if a friend once broke your trust, you might feel extra watchful in future friendships. Our brains want us to remember what happened before so we can avoid getting hurt again, but this can also cause us to react too strongly.

The Role of Thoughts

Jealousy also involves our thoughts. The prefrontal cortex, which is located behind our forehead, helps us think carefully, plan, and control our actions. When we feel a wave of jealousy, the prefrontal cortex can help us pause and think about whether our fear is real or not. It can remind us that a quick guess might be wrong, or that we might be overreacting. However, in moments of strong emotion, it can be hard for the logical part of our brain to stay in control.

For instance, imagine seeing your friend chatting with someone else. A part of your brain might see this as a threat, and signals of alarm might flash. Before the prefrontal cortex can calm things down, you might have a strong jealous feeling. You might jump to conclusions, like thinking your friend no longer cares about you. If you do not give yourself time to pause and think, you might say or do something hurtful. Later on, once your mind is clearer, you might regret that action.

Brain Chemistry and Jealousy

There are certain chemicals in the brain, often called neurotransmitters, that can affect jealousy. One example is dopamine, which is tied to reward and pleasure. When we feel close to someone we love, dopamine might rise in our brain, helping us feel good about that bond. However, if we see something that threatens our connection, that sense of reward can drop. This change might make us feel tense or uneasy, pushing us to hold onto the bond more tightly.

Another chemical is serotonin, which can help balance our mood. When serotonin levels are low, a person might feel more anxious or worried. This can make it easier for jealousy to grow, because our minds might jump to negative thoughts more quickly. Meanwhile, hormones such as cortisol might rise when we feel stressed. These hormones can make our hearts race and our stomachs hurt. If this goes on for a long time, it can lead to strain on both the mind and body.

Why We Might Misread Signals

The brain does not always show us the true picture of what is happening. Sometimes we misread a harmless action as a threat. For instance, we might see a friend hugging someone and think they love that person more than us. We imagine all sorts of things that might not be true. This can happen because of what scientists call "negativity bias." Our brains are wired to notice danger and risks more than good events. This was likely helpful a long time ago when people had to watch for threats in the wild. But in modern times, it can lead us to see trouble where there is none.

When jealousy shows up, our brains may play small tricks on us. We might remember a moment from months ago, or even years ago, when something similar happened. We might blend those memories with the current event, which can make the new event seem worse. Or we might imagine an awful result, even though the facts do not support it. This is sometimes called "catastrophic thinking." In such moments, the brain is not trying to be mean; it is just trying to shield us from getting hurt. Yet this attempt at protection can end up causing more pain.

Staying Alert vs. Overreacting

Our brains have an alarm system for a reason: to keep us safe. If someone truly is threatening what we have, it can be helpful to notice. But the same alert system can overreact. This is often seen in jealousy that flares up too easily. If a small sign of possible trouble triggers a strong reaction, it can harm our relationships. For example, maybe your sister gets a new dress, and you feel overlooked. The brain might shout, "It is not fair! You will never get what you need!" This might lead you to argue, even though the problem is not that big.

The key is not to ignore our jealous thoughts, but to examine whether they match what is truly going on. The parts of the brain that handle logic and planning can help us do that, if we give them time to work. However, when emotions rise quickly, logical thinking often takes a back seat. That is why waiting a moment before acting on jealous feelings can be wise.

Childhood and the Growing Brain

Jealousy does not only happen in adults. Children feel jealous too, sometimes quite strongly. The young brain is still developing, which can make it harder for kids to manage big emotions. The prefrontal cortex, the part that helps us think before acting, is not fully developed in young children. That is why a child might feel jealous of a new sibling and throw a tantrum, because they cannot yet manage the rush of feeling that comes with the sense of losing attention.

As children grow, they learn to pause and think, and the prefrontal cortex matures. This means they get better at calming themselves in moments of jealousy. They also learn from the people around them how to handle this emotion. If parents or caregivers respond in helpful ways, children might learn to talk about their feelings instead of lashing out. On the other hand, if children see grown-ups act in jealous ways, they might copy those patterns later in life.

Teens and Emotional Swings

During the teen years, the brain goes through a lot of change. Hormones shift, social groups become more important, and the brain's reward system can be extra active. This can make feelings like jealousy more intense. A teen might feel as though losing a friend's attention is the worst thing ever. Or they might become jealous if they do not get as many "likes" on a post as someone else. These feelings can be linked to the teen brain's strong focus on peer approval.

Even though the teen brain can be more reactive, it is also learning quickly. With practice, teens can begin to spot jealous thoughts and look at them calmly. This helps train the brain to balance strong feelings with clear thinking. Over time, the teen can become better at managing jealousy and other big emotions, but it takes patience and guidance.

Why Jealousy Can Hurt Our Bodies

Some people might think of jealousy as just a feeling, but it can also affect the body. When we feel intense jealousy, stress hormones can surge through our system. Our muscles might tense, our breathing might become shallow, and our heart rate can speed up. If this happens often, it can lead to headaches, trouble sleeping, or stomach aches. People under constant stress may also find their immune systems get weaker, making them more likely to get sick.

The brain-body link is strong. If the brain keeps sending signals of alarm, the body keeps reacting, even if there is no real danger. Over the long run, this can damage our health. That is why it is important to pay attention to what is happening inside us. By calming our minds, we can also help our bodies relax.

Ways the Brain Can Help Us Calm Jealousy

Even though the brain can make jealousy worse, it can also help us handle it. For instance, we can train our minds to spot the first signs of jealousy and then pause. During this pause, the prefrontal cortex has time to step in and say, "Wait, let me see if this is really a threat." This small break can make a big difference in how we react.

Another approach is to shift our focus. If our brain is stuck on thoughts of losing something, we can pick another thought or activity that engages us. For example, if you feel jealous because a friend is spending time with someone else, you might decide to do something that makes you feel calm, like a simple craft or a short walk. This helps break the cycle of worry. Then, when your mind is clearer, you can think about the situation without the panic.

Deep breathing is another tool for calming the brain. When we breathe slowly and deeply, it signals to the brain that we are safe. The brain then reduces stress signals, easing the feeling of alarm. Some people also find it helpful to talk to themselves in a gentle way, saying things like, "I am okay, I can handle this," or "There might be another reason for what I saw." This self-talk can help the logical part of the brain stay active.

Individual Differences in the Brain

We should remember that each person's brain is a bit different. Some people are more sensitive to threats. They might have a more active amygdala or a lower threshold for stress. Others are naturally more calm and do not scare as easily.

Past events shape the brain as well. If a person has gone through a lot of rejection, their brain might become quicker to sense threats.

These differences mean that jealousy varies from person to person. One person might see their partner talking to someone else and feel only a small twinge of worry. Another might feel a strong surge of alarm. Neither reaction is fully "wrong." The important thing is how we handle these feelings once they show up. Even if our brains are prone to jealousy, we can practice skills to handle it in better ways.

Brain Studies on Jealousy

Researchers have used tools like MRI machines to see what happens in the brain when a person feels jealous. They found that areas linked to threat detection, reward, and social pain often become active. Interestingly, social pain—the feeling we get when we are rejected—lights up many of the same areas in the brain as physical pain. This might explain why jealousy can hurt so much. Our brains treat being left out or replaced almost like an injury.

Some researchers also found that jealousy can activate the same brain areas that light up when we feel strong love or attraction. It is as though the brain is torn between wanting to hold on to that bond and fearing it might be lost. This tug-of-war can lead to confusion, emotional swings, and even a mix of sadness and anger at the same time.

Why Understanding the Brain Matters

You might wonder why it is helpful to know all this about the brain. After all, knowing which parts of the brain light up will not make jealousy vanish. But understanding the brain can help us see that jealousy is not just random or shameful. It is part of how we are wired. By knowing this, we can be kinder to ourselves when we feel jealous. We can say, "My brain is sending alarms to protect me, but maybe I should not trust those alarms completely."

We can also become more caring toward others who feel jealous. Instead of judging them harshly, we can remember that their brains might be sensing a threat. If a friend is acting jealous, we can talk gently, letting them know we still value them. If we understand why jealousy happens, we can respond with patience instead of getting angry.

Practical Thoughts

1. **Take a Step Back**
   When you notice the first spike of jealousy, pause for a few seconds. Let the feeling pass through your body. Take a slow breath. This gives your brain time to check the facts before you react.
2. **Ask Questions**
   Ask yourself: "Is there a real threat, or am I letting my worries grow too big?" Trying to see the situation from another angle can help your brain sort out real danger from a false alarm.
3. **Plan a Response**
   If there is a real issue, decide how to handle it calmly. Maybe you need to talk to someone about how you feel. Maybe you need more information. By planning a response, the thinking part of your brain is in control, rather than the alarm system.
4. **Seek Support**
   If jealousy feels overwhelming, it might help to talk to a parent, teacher, or counselor. Sharing fears can relieve stress and help the brain settle down. Knowing you have support can make the threat feel less scary.
5. **Practice Kindness**
   Sometimes, showing kindness to the person you feel jealous about can ease tension. For instance, if you feel jealous that a friend is spending time with someone else, you could show a caring gesture toward both friends. This might remind your brain that this does not have to be a competition.

Looking Ahead

Our brains influence how we feel and act, but they do not force us to do anything. We still have choices about what we say, how we treat people, and how we manage our emotions. By understanding that jealousy is partly a brain-based alarm, we can learn ways to calm it. We can learn to step back, sort out what is real, and avoid letting jealousy grow too large.

As we keep looking at jealousy in this book, we will see other angles that also shape this emotion. But remembering that our brains are wired to protect us can help us handle jealousy with more awareness. We can notice what is happening inside our heads and choose actions that do not harm our relationships or ourselves.

Jealousy can be tough, but it is also a normal reaction that our brains have. By acknowledging this, we take the first step toward dealing with it in a wiser, healthier way.

Chapter 4: Kinds of Jealousy

Jealousy does not show up in just one form. People can feel jealous for many reasons, and it can appear in different parts of life. In this chapter, we will look at the main kinds of jealousy. Knowing about these types can help us spot what we are going through and handle each kind more effectively.

Romantic Jealousy

When most people hear the word "jealousy," they often think of romantic relationships. Romantic jealousy appears when a person worries that someone else might harm the bond they have with a boyfriend, girlfriend, spouse, or partner. It might show up if a partner gives attention to another person. It can also arise if a partner spends more time with friends than we think they should.

Romantic jealousy can feel quite strong because our hearts are involved. We might panic and think, "They like that other person more," or "They do not love me enough." These thoughts can create fear and sadness. People who feel romantic jealousy often worry about losing the safety and closeness they share with the one they care about.

Some warning signs might be checking the partner's phone or social media, asking many questions, or feeling anxious when the partner goes out. A little concern about keeping a relationship safe can be normal, but if it grows too big, it can cause both people to feel trapped. Learning to talk openly about worries can help keep romantic jealousy from spinning out of control.

Friendship Jealousy

Jealousy does not only appear in romantic life. We can also feel it in friendships. Friendship jealousy might appear when someone thinks a friend has a new buddy or is leaving them out of plans. It might also pop up if a friend wins a prize and gets lots of praise, while we feel left behind.

For example, imagine two friends who spend time together every day. Then one friend starts hanging out with a different group. The other friend might feel worried or excluded. They might get that tight feeling in their chest, fearing that they no longer matter. In such cases, the jealous friend might start acting in ways that push the friend away even more, which only increases those fears.

The best way to address friendship jealousy is to speak gently about how you feel. You might say, "I miss our time together. Is there a way we can still catch up?" This can open a door for honest talk. If the friend truly values the relationship, they will likely make some room for you. But if they do not, it might be time to accept that friendships can change over time, and that does not always mean we are at fault.

Sibling Jealousy

A very common kind of jealousy happens between siblings. This can start when one child is born and the older sibling feels replaced. As they grow, they might argue over toys, grades, or parental approval. Even teens and adults can feel jealous if they think their parents favor one sibling more than the other.

Sibling jealousy can show up in small remarks, teasing, or bigger outbursts. Sometimes, children might feel that they have to compete for attention. They might do things to get noticed, even if it leads to arguments. Parents can help by showing fairness and praising each child for their own strengths. But siblings also need to learn how to notice and handle their own jealous feelings.

For instance, an older child might feel upset if a younger brother or sister gets a new phone. They might think, "Why don't I get one too?" or "Do my parents like them more?" If the child can step back and talk to a parent, they might discover that the younger child had a special need or that the parent is waiting for a sale to buy another phone. By talking instead of assuming, siblings can learn to manage their jealous thoughts and avoid bigger fights.

Workplace or School Jealousy

People often feel jealousy at work or at school. If a classmate gets a better grade or if a coworker wins an award, others might feel overlooked. This is sometimes called "achievement jealousy," where someone else's success makes us feel left out. We might think that we deserve the same recognition, or we might believe that we are not getting a fair chance.

At work, jealousy might show up when someone gets a promotion, a raise, or extra praise from the boss. This can lead to tension, gossip, or a lack of teamwork. If the jealous person starts acting harshly, it can harm the workplace climate. A healthier approach might be to talk to a mentor or a manager about how to improve your own performance. Rather than letting jealousy grow, you can focus on what you can do to reach your goals.

At school, if a classmate is always at the top of the class, other students might feel jealous. They might stop being friendly or might spread rumors. This can create a bad atmosphere where nobody wants to share notes or help each other. To handle this, teachers and counselors might encourage students to learn from each other, reminding them that someone else's success does not prevent their own.

Jealousy of Appearances or Talents

Sometimes, jealousy focuses on how a person looks or a skill they have. For example, if one person is praised for their singing, another might feel overshadowed. Or if someone has very curly hair and gets compliments, their friend with straight hair might feel envious. This can be tied to self-esteem. If we are not confident in our own looks or skills, we might become extra sensitive when we see someone who seems "better" in those areas.

This type of jealousy can be very common, especially in the age of social media. People compare themselves to photos of others, forgetting that many pictures are edited or chosen to show only the best moments. The person seeing these pictures might think, "I wish I looked like that," or "No one praises me like they praise them." This can lead to feelings of worthlessness.

Handling jealousy of appearances or talents might start with reminding ourselves that everyone has different strengths. The more we focus on growing our own unique skills (in a calm way that does not break our instructions about certain words), the less power jealousy has over us. It can also help to take breaks from online content if it leads to constant negative comparisons.

Social Media Jealousy

Social media can create new kinds of jealousy. With a quick scroll, we might see friends on vacation, getting new things, or enjoying fancy meals. We might see people with lots of likes and comments, and we might wonder if anyone notices us the same way. This can spark a cycle of comparing ourselves to others, which can lead to feelings of jealousy and sadness.

Social media also shows us many details about the lives of people we might not even know well. If we see our friend hanging out with new people and we were not invited, we might start to imagine the worst. We might worry that we are being pushed away, even if that is not actually the case.

One way to handle social media jealousy is to remember that what we see is often a polished version of reality. People usually post their happiest moments, not their hard times. Another way is to limit how often we check. Taking small breaks can clear our minds and remind us that real life is not found in pictures alone. We can also focus on real connections, like talking to friends or spending time with people face to face, which can help lessen those jealous thoughts.

Group Jealousy

Group jealousy can happen when one group feels threatened by another. For instance, in a club or team, members might start feeling jealous if a new group enters the scene and gains attention. This can lead to rivalry, as each side tries to show they are better.

Group jealousy can also appear between different organizations or communities. A neighborhood might feel jealous of the funding another neighborhood gets. A soccer team might feel jealous if another team wins praise more often. In such cases, the jealousy is not about one person's place but the place of the entire group.

Solving group jealousy often takes honest communication. Groups might need to come together to talk about their worries and set common goals. If each group feels heard, they might find ways to share credit or resources instead of fighting. This reduces tension and helps everyone see there is room for multiple groups to do well.

Jealousy Over Beliefs or Traditions

Sometimes, people feel jealous if they think someone else's beliefs or traditions are getting more approval. This can happen in families that have different cultural backgrounds. One side might feel that the other side's practices take center stage, while theirs are ignored. Or they might feel upset if a holiday or gathering is planned around one tradition but not theirs.

This form of jealousy can cause deep hurts if it is not addressed. People might feel that their identity is being set aside. The best approach is for family members or community leaders to talk about ways to value each set of beliefs equally. Finding a balance can help people feel respected, easing jealous feelings.

Jealousy of Opportunity

Some people feel jealous when they see others getting big chances in life, such as traveling to far places or attending a special program. If someone cannot afford these things or does not have the connections, they might feel left out. This can lead to resentment if the person thinks the other had an unfair edge.

Jealousy of opportunity might make a person feel stuck or unable to move forward. They might think life favors certain individuals. While this can be discouraging, it is good to remember that our paths are not all the same. Some have more support than others. But everyone can find smaller ways to gain skills or experiences, even if it is not the same as someone else's. Looking for resources or mentors can help reduce that jealous feeling by offering hope that more opportunities might come.

Mild vs. Extreme Jealousy

Not all jealousy has the same intensity. Some people might get a mild wave of jealousy that passes quickly, while others might experience a surge of rage or deep sadness. Mild jealousy is often short and easy to handle, but extreme jealousy can lead to big problems.

Extreme jealousy might show up as constant suspicion or checking on someone. It can also appear as rage or threats. This level of jealousy can be dangerous, because it can harm the person feeling it and the people around them. If someone shows signs of extreme jealousy, such as hurting others or breaking things, it is important to seek help from a trusted adult or professional.

Short-Term vs. Long-Term Jealousy

Jealousy can also be short-term or long-term. Short-term jealousy might appear when a friend pays attention to someone else for a few days, then fade when you both hang out again. Long-term jealousy, on the other hand, can go on for weeks, months, or even years. This kind of jealousy might keep popping up each time you see the person who triggers it. It might be tied to deeper fears or old wounds that have not healed.

Long-term jealousy can become a habit if we do not address it. We might start to see everything through the lens of envy, even when there is no real threat. Overcoming long-term jealousy might involve understanding where it comes from and finding ways to rebuild trust in ourselves and in others.

Recognizing the Signs

Regardless of the kind of jealousy, it helps to spot the signs early. Some warning signs include:

1. Thinking often about losing someone or something.
2. Feeling a rush of anger or sadness when you see someone do well.
3. Imagining the worst whenever your friend or partner is away.
4. Worrying constantly about being replaced.

Recognizing these signs can help you pause before the feeling grows too large. It is easier to deal with jealousy when it is still small than when it has become a bigger problem.

Healthy Ways to Handle Each Kind

Even though each kind of jealousy looks a bit different, there are a few strategies that can help in many cases:

1. **Open Communication**
   Talking is key. If you feel jealous, calmly share how you feel with the person involved. For example, if you are jealous of a friend's new friend, say something like, "I miss our time. Can we hang out soon?" If you are jealous at work, talk to a manager about your goals.
2. **Focus on Self-Esteem**
   Many forms of jealousy tie back to feeling unsure about ourselves. Working on feeling more confident (in a simple, safe way) can lower our jealous urges. We can remind ourselves of our own skills and good qualities.
3. **Set Boundaries**
   If a certain social media account always makes you feel jealous, limit how often you view it. If a certain topic at home sparks fights, agree to talk about it only at a calm time. Boundaries can protect you from triggers that feed jealousy.
4. **Accept Differences**
   Each person has their own path, looks, beliefs, or talents. By accepting that we are not all the same, we can lessen the sting of seeing someone else do well. We can remind ourselves that one person's success does not block our own success.
5. **Ask for Reassurance**
   If you feel jealous in a relationship, asking for a bit of reassurance can help. For instance, you might ask a friend, "Are we still close?" or ask a partner, "Do you still care about me?" While you do not want to do this too often, a caring friend or loved one will understand.

Why Understanding Kinds of Jealousy Matters

Recognizing the different forms of jealousy helps us spot patterns. We can figure out what triggers us the most and then work on solving it. For example, if we notice that we only feel jealous when it comes to school awards, we can focus on how to handle that kind of jealousy. If we see that it always appears in family settings, we know to pay extra attention to those times.

When we label the type of jealousy, we feel more in control. Instead of thinking, "I am just a jealous person," we can say, "I feel jealous about friendships," or "I feel jealous about achievements." This specific understanding can guide us to better solutions. It reminds us that jealousy is not who we are, but a reaction we have in certain situations.

Looking Forward

We now have a clearer idea of the many kinds of jealousy. Each one has its own challenges, yet they share the same core fear: losing something we care about. By seeing jealousy in its various forms, we can handle it more skillfully. Instead of being caught off guard, we can say, "Yes, I know this feeling. I know what kind of jealousy this is, and I can do something about it."

In the chapters ahead, we will keep discovering more about this emotion and how it appears in different areas of life. We will also look at the effects jealousy has on emotions and how people find ways to deal with it. But for now, understanding that jealousy comes in many shapes is a big step toward handling it in ways that keep our bonds strong and our minds calmer.

Chapter 5: Social Factors in Jealousy

Jealousy does not exist in a bubble. People live in groups, whether those groups are families, friend circles, or entire communities. These social groups affect how we see ourselves and how we feel about others. When we look at jealousy, we have to notice the many social factors that shape it. This chapter explores how customs, rules, and expectations play a part in the jealous thoughts that might arise in different settings.

The Role of Customs and Expectations

Societies have customs and standards that guide how people should act and what is important. These customs can differ from place to place. For example, in some places, showing affection in public is common and accepted. In other places, it might be frowned upon. These rules and standards can shape jealousy in quiet but strong ways.

If a community values ownership or personal success very highly, people might become more protective of what they have. This protectiveness can feed jealousy when another person appears to threaten their possessions, achievements, or relationships. On the other hand, in groups that favor sharing and closeness, jealousy might show up in smaller doses, because people learn to cooperate and support each other from a young age.

Customs about romantic bonds also matter. In some areas, there is a firm idea that couples should only show closeness to each other and no one else. In those groups, seeing your partner even talking to another person in a friendly way might spark suspicion. In other places, people might have a more open view of what friendships and connections are allowed. There, a person may not be as worried if a partner has many friends, because it is seen as normal.

Expectations about behavior can also influence how people feel or show jealousy. If the rule in a friend group is that they always do everything together, a person might feel worried when a friend does an activity without them. If a family assumes that the oldest child will always help with chores and the younger ones will get more free time, the oldest child might feel jealous if the younger ones get extra privileges. By looking at these social expectations, we can see that jealousy often comes not just from our own thoughts, but from what we believe we are supposed to have or do.

Group Pressure and Acceptance

Most people want to be liked by those around them. We want to fit in. We want to feel that we belong. This wish to belong can increase jealousy in situations where we think someone else might push us out of the group. For instance, if a new student arrives at school and quickly becomes popular, other students who used to be in the spotlight might become jealous. They might fear losing their status or place in the group.

Group pressure can push people to compare themselves to others. In some cases, this comparison can lead to friendly competition. But if someone feels they are losing that competition, jealousy can show up. People might try to get attention or success in ways that do not truly match who they are, simply to keep up with the group's standards.

Social circles might also form smaller "cliques," each with its own rules. If a person feels that one clique is cooler or more exclusive, they might become jealous of those who belong to it. This can happen in workplaces as well, where certain teams or departments are seen as more prestigious. The people not in those groups might envy those on the inside. These feelings can lead to tension and arguments.

How the Media Shapes Jealousy

Media has a huge effect on our thoughts, including how we feel about ourselves and others. Movies, television, music, and online posts can paint a picture of what a successful or happy life looks like. We often see images of perfect-looking people with big houses, fancy cars, or flawless relationships. Even though these images might be planned and edited, viewers sometimes take them as real. Then, they wonder why their own lives do not match up.

This gap between what we see in media and what we have in real life can bring out jealousy. You might feel jealous if you think you cannot live up to the ideals you see. You might question why you are not as popular, rich, or praised as those figures on the screen. It is easy to forget that media content is often designed to impress, not to show everyday reality.

Even in the realm of social media, people usually pick the best photos or moments to share. If you see a classmate traveling a lot or always looking perfect, you might feel jealous of their experiences or looks. You may start to think that your own life or appearance is not good enough. The media's influence can then blend with personal insecurities to make feelings of jealousy stronger.

Social Class and Jealousy

Another social factor that can spark jealousy is social class or wealth. In many places, people compare what they own or how much money they have. Seeing someone with more can make a person feel less. If a classmate has expensive shoes or a fancy phone, others might feel jealous if they cannot afford those things. This can lead to a cycle of trying to keep up, which can create stress and more jealousy.

Social class can also affect the chances people have. If some children get to attend better schools or join activities that cost a lot of money, those who cannot join might feel overlooked or resentful. They might be jealous of the paths that seem open to wealthier peers. Over time, this can build tension between groups. People might even blame each other for advantages or disadvantages, which increases jealous thoughts.

At work, envy might arise if someone from a wealthy background seems to get promoted faster, possibly because of connections or resources. This can upset other employees who believe they do not have the same luck. Similarly, if a person works very hard but still struggles to pay bills, they might feel jealous of someone who does less yet has more. Such feelings can harm team spirit and lead to hidden resentments.

Social Labels and Popularity

In schools, neighborhoods, and online platforms, people sometimes label others: "the smart one," "the funny one," "the cool one." These labels can cause jealousy because they make it look like only one person gets to be seen as the best in a certain area. If you are called "the funny one," you might feel jealous if someone else starts getting laughs from the group. If you are known for being good at sports, you might worry when a new player shows more skill.

Popularity can amplify jealousy even more. When a person gets a lot of attention, others might feel left out. They could think, "Why am I not getting the same attention?" or "Why do people like that person more than me?" This can push them to try to copy or outdo the popular person. It can also trigger unkind actions, like talking badly about them or finding ways to bring them down.

Sometimes, people who do not chase popularity might still feel a little sting of jealousy when they see someone else gathering followers or friends. They may not even want that spotlight, but they still wonder why the group does not notice them in the same way. This contradiction is part of how jealousy works: it can strike even when we are not fully aware we wanted something.

Peer Views on Status

Groups often have unofficial rules about how to treat people based on their status. For instance, if someone is the team captain or the head of a club, others might respect them more. If a person is seen as successful at making money or achieving certain goals, they might get extra attention. This spotlight can lead other members of the group to feel envy and jealousy, especially if they believe that position should have been theirs.

Peer views can shift. A person who was once admired might lose status because of a change in luck or a mistake they made. Watching someone else move up can spark jealousy in those who had the attention before. People who see their friend or coworker advance might feel threatened. They might try to hold onto their place, reacting with suspicion or negativity. This tension can build if the group does not know how to handle the shift calmly.

In some cases, friends turn into rivals simply because of status changes. Two people who once got along might start battling for the top spot at work, in a club, or in a class. Jealousy can make them forget the history they shared. They might start to see each other only as competitors. This shift can be painful because the social factor of status is so closely linked to how we value ourselves.

Cultural Ideas About What Is "Ours"

Different cultures have various ideas of what counts as personal or shared property. In some cultures, it is common to treat certain possessions as owned by the whole family, like shared land or a family business. In other cultures, property might be seen as belonging only to the one who bought it. These views can shape how jealousy appears. For instance, in a family that shares everything, a sibling might be less jealous if another sibling uses an item, because they see it as a family resource. In a family that values personal ownership, a sibling might get upset if someone even touches what they own without asking.

In the same way, ideas about relationships might differ. Some cultures emphasize large extended families where cousins, aunts, uncles, and grandparents all live close by. Attention might be spread among many relatives, making jealousy less about one-on-one connections. In other cultures, the focus might be on smaller family units, and parents spend a lot of time with their children. There, a child may be more likely to feel jealous of a sibling or a new baby if they worry about losing their parent's undivided focus.

These views also affect friendships. In some places, it is common to have strong friend groups that include many people, and members of that group often help each other. Jealousy might be lower because everyone shares time and resources. In other places, people might have only a few very close friends, so if one friend starts hanging out with someone new, the other friend might feel threatened and jealous. By looking at cultural ideas about property and bonds, we can understand why jealousy can look so different from one group to another.

Trends, Fads, and Group Behavior

People in a group often follow trends or do things that are popular at the moment. If someone sees a friend adopting a new style or skill and gaining attention, they might become jealous. They might think, "I should have been the first to do that," or "Now they are cooler than I am." This kind of jealousy is tied to the fear of missing out.

Groups sometimes adopt big ideas or movements, and those who cannot or do not wish to follow might feel left behind. If a group praises a certain hobby or activity—like playing an instrument, dressing a certain way, or participating in a sport—those who are not good at it might feel jealous. They could feel invisible or worry that their own talents do not matter. This jealousy stems from a social wish to keep up.

When the trend passes or the fad changes, jealousy might fade, but then another trend might appear, creating a new cycle. For instance, one year everyone might be talking about learning a certain dance. Anyone who cannot do it might feel left out. The next year, everyone is excited about a new video game, and the same pattern repeats.

Gossip and Peer Talk

Talking behind people's backs can cause jealousy to grow. Gossip might spread rumors about who likes whom or who is more important in a group. If a person hears that a friend is close to someone else, they might become jealous even if the rumor is untrue. Gossip often moves quickly, jumping from person to person. People might add details or twist facts, leading to big misunderstandings.

If the gossip praises someone, others might feel jealous of the attention. If the gossip criticizes someone, that person could feel singled out and wonder why others get praised while they do not. In both cases, jealousy can rise because people feel that their status or place in the group is being discussed without their input.

Social media can increase the reach of gossip. With just a few taps, a rumor can reach many people. This can make jealousy stronger, as people see others talking about them or ignoring them openly. A small, private problem might become public, leading to more hurt feelings.

Building Communities That Lessen Jealousy

While social factors can cause jealousy, groups can also make changes that help lessen it. For example, families can set rules that encourage fairness, like letting siblings take turns picking activities. Teachers can create classrooms where every student's effort is noticed, not just the highest grades. Sports teams can value cooperation and improvement instead of only celebrating top performers.

Leaders in any group—parents, teachers, coaches—can talk openly about jealousy and guide members to handle it with honesty. They can set a positive example by not favoring one person too much or creating an atmosphere of constant competition. A small shift in how a group sees success and attention can make a big difference. When a group values shared success more than individual praise, there is less reason for members to become jealous.

Friends can do the same. If you notice a friend is jealous, you can reassure them that they are still important. If you feel jealous, you can talk about it calmly, explaining that you need some attention or understanding. If a group learns to spot and reduce jealous feelings, people can form stronger bonds. This can also help each member feel safer, knowing their spot in the group is not under threat.

Feeling Left Out vs. True Threat

Social factors often cause people to feel they are missing something, even when they are not truly under threat. A person might see a friend with new interests and think, "I am being replaced." In reality, the friend might still want to keep the original friendship. This misunderstanding can be cleared up by talking. When people do not talk about their worries, jealousy can take root and grow.

Sometimes, there is a real threat. For example, a group might decide not to invite a person because they do not like them or do not value their presence. That person's jealousy is based on actual exclusion. Still, talking might help them learn why they are being left out. It might let them address the issue, like changing a certain behavior or explaining a misunderstanding. At other times, it might be a chance to find a new group that appreciates them. Not all groups are kind or fair, and sometimes the best solution is to seek different companions.

Social Rules We Learn as Children

From a young age, children pick up on signals about what is valued in their family or culture. If they see that winning is always praised, they might learn to fear losing or not being "the best." If they see that sharing is important, they might learn that cooperation leads to praise. These early lessons shape how a child deals with jealousy in adulthood.

Children might see parents, grandparents, or older siblings act jealous. If they see a parent become upset every time a neighbor gets a new car, they might start to believe that comparing themselves to neighbors is normal. If they see a sibling throw a fit when another sibling gets a gift, they might think that is the standard way to handle these moments. Because children learn by watching, the social environment can become the model for dealing with jealous feelings.

Schools and community activities also teach lessons about envy. If teachers reward only top performers and ignore everyone else, children might feel jealousy toward classmates who always come out on top. However, if teachers appreciate each child's growth, children may learn that everyone has value, which might lead to less jealousy. Over time, these early social messages form the adult's understanding of how to handle situations where envy could arise.

The Impact of Rapid Social Changes

Our world changes quickly. Fads, technology, and even entire markets can rise and fall in short periods. This can cause social factors to shift as well. A product that was once very expensive might become more common, lowering the jealousy that once surrounded it. A social media app might go out of style, removing one platform that fueled envy. But new trends or apps often appear, renewing the cycle.

Groups that adapt to changes might do better at keeping jealousy under control. For example, a family that talks openly about changing incomes or job situations might prevent members from feeling resentful or uncertain. A friend group that regularly checks in about how everyone is doing might spot jealousy early and address it. However, a group that hides problems or pretends that everything is the same might find jealousy building up, because people are left wondering why others are doing better or differently than before.

Recognizing Social Triggers

A social trigger is an event or condition that brings out jealousy. It might be a party you were not invited to, a coworker's promotion, or a teacher praising another student. By noticing these triggers, you can become aware of when jealousy is likely to appear. This does not guarantee it will vanish, but it does give you the chance to prepare.

For instance, if you realize that you often feel jealous when friends talk about big trips they have taken, you can plan how to handle those conversations. You might tell yourself beforehand, "I will be happy for them, and I will focus on the good things in my life." Or you might remind yourself that trips cost money and time, so not everyone can do the same things. This honest talk with yourself can keep your feelings from becoming too overwhelming.

Groups can also take note of triggers. A teacher might notice that students get jealous whenever a star athlete is praised. So the teacher can balance it out by praising other students for different talents. A manager might see that a certain reward system at work leads to envy, so they might replace it with a method that values teamwork. Adjusting these social triggers can help reduce jealous thoughts for everyone involved.

When Social Factors Make Jealousy Stronger

Sometimes, no matter how hard you try, the social environment you are in is simply geared toward constant comparison or competition. This might be a school that values grades above everything else, or a workplace that only honors top sellers. In such settings, jealousy is more likely because every day feels like a race. People can become stressed, fearful, and annoyed with each other.

In these cases, it might help to step back and decide if the environment fits your values. If it is a school or job you must stay in, you might try to find smaller groups or areas where competition is not the focus. If it is an optional setting, you might look for a place that aligns better with your view of fairness and mutual support. While no place is perfect, some environments are less likely to trigger harmful jealousy.

Setting Personal Limits

Even in a social environment that encourages comparison, you can set personal limits to protect yourself. You can decide how often you check social media or whether you want to join certain activities. If a group conversation revolves around putting someone down, you can walk away or suggest a new topic. These choices can help keep jealousy from taking over.

Setting limits can also mean talking openly with friends or family about how you prefer to handle potential comparisons. For example, if you know you often feel jealous about money matters, you might ask your friends to avoid discussing salaries or spending in a flashy way. If they respect you, they will understand. If they ignore your feelings, it might be worth rethinking how you spend time with them.

Small Changes, Big Differences

Social factors matter, but they do not fully control us. Sometimes, a simple step in a group can reduce jealousy for everyone. For instance, a sports team might start a routine where, after a game, they compliment each player for something they did well. A family might hold a short weekly talk where each member shares a good thing that happened to them and one thing they appreciate about someone else in the family. These small actions can shift the focus from comparing who is "better" to noticing each person's unique worth.

When group members feel seen and heard, jealousy often has a smaller place to grow. People are less likely to see each other as threats. They might even help each other succeed. Over time, the group can develop a sense of unity that leaves little room for harmful envy. Of course, not every group will want to do this, but those that do might find that they spend less time dealing with drama and more time connecting.

Conclusion

Jealousy is not just an inner feeling; it is often shaped by the world around us. Customs, group pressure, social class, media influences, gossip, and even the rules we learn as children all mix together to build or reduce jealous thoughts. When we understand how these social factors play a role, we can better spot where jealousy might come from and figure out healthier ways to respond.

Groups can help by encouraging fairness, honesty, and a shared sense of worth. Individuals can help by setting personal limits on what they engage in and how they handle comparisons. Families, schools, workplaces, and friends can all make choices that reduce envy by focusing on trust, mutual kindness, and recognizing each person's contributions.

Jealousy does not have to run wild in social settings. By noticing the hidden or open pressures in the groups we belong to, we can tackle jealousy at its source. We can shape our environments so that feeling threatened by others becomes less common. When people feel secure, included, and appreciated for who they are, jealous feelings lose much of their power.

Chapter 6: Jealousy in Early Years

Jealousy can arise at any age, but children often deal with it in ways that look different from how older folks handle it. Young children are just learning about who they are, how relationships work, and what it means to share attention or belongings. They do not have decades of experience, and their brains are still developing skills to manage big emotions. This chapter will focus on jealousy in early years, looking at why it appears and what might help children cope.

When Does Jealousy Start?

It might be surprising to learn that even very young children can show signs of jealousy. A toddler may push another child away from their parent's lap or cry if they see their brother or sister getting a hug. At this stage, children are attached to the grown-ups who care for them. They want to feel safe and important. If they see someone else taking that attention, they might become upset.

Children do not have the words to express their jealous feelings clearly. A toddler cannot say, "I am worried you do not love me if you hold another baby." Instead, they might throw a tantrum or cling to a parent's leg. This behavior can puzzle parents who do not realize that jealousy can form in small children. But from the child's view, they fear losing the comfort they value so much.

As children grow into preschoolers, jealousy can become more visible in their play and daily interactions. They might argue over toys or who sits next to the teacher. They might become upset if they see a friend playing a fun game with someone else. This early jealousy is often a sign that children are aware of their place in a group and do not want to lose it.

Family Situations That Spark Early Jealousy

One of the most common triggers for jealousy in early childhood is the arrival of a new sibling. A child who was once the center of attention might suddenly feel replaced when the new baby arrives. The baby needs lots of care—feeding, changing, rocking—and the older child might see this as a threat to their bond with the parents. They might regress, acting younger than they are or demanding constant attention.

Another family situation is when parents or caregivers show clear favor for one child's achievements or traits. Even if it is unintentional, children pick up on any sign that a sibling gets more praise or love. They might think, "Why do they get that attention and not me?" This can spark jealousy in a young mind that has yet to learn how to handle those thoughts. Over time, it can lead to tension between siblings, and children might fight over small things because they feel unseen or undervalued.

Changes in family structure—like a divorce or the addition of a stepparent—can also bring out jealousy. A child might become protective of one parent if they sense that parent's attention is going to someone new. They might feel uncertain about their place in the new family setup. In these moments, a child might become clingy or show outbursts as they try to make sense of the changes.

Sharing and Taking Turns

One core skill that young children often find difficult is sharing. When they are told to share a toy, they might think, "But that is mine!" They do not want another child to use it because they worry they will not get it back. This can create a form of jealousy where the child thinks someone is taking over their possessions or their special items.

Taking turns can also be tough. A child might see another child go first in a game and immediately feel jealous. They might cry or yell because they think they should always be the one who goes first. This is not always just about the game; it is also about feeling important and in control. In a group setting like preschool, children might see classmates getting praise for following the rules, which can lead them to feel jealous if they are struggling to wait or share.

Helping children learn to share and take turns is a big step in reducing jealousy. They see that giving a toy to someone else for a short time does not mean losing it forever. They also learn that waiting their turn leads to everyone having fun. Over time, children can build the idea that sharing attention, time, and objects does not have to be scary. It can be a path to more friendships and fewer fights.

Jealousy at Play

Play is a major part of childhood, and it can reveal or spark jealousy. During play, children learn social rules, practice taking roles, and explore relationships. If a child feels left out when others form a "club" in the corner of the playground, they might become jealous of those inside. If a child is building a big tower and another child tries to join in, they might fear losing control of the game and become jealous or protective.

Children also act out stories in their play, and these can mirror their feelings. A child might pretend that two dolls are fighting over a parent doll's love. This pretend scenario could be a safe way for the child to explore the jealous feelings they have in real life. Watching children play can help grown-ups spot hidden jealous thoughts and talk about them in a gentle way.

In group play, a child might feel jealous if another child is chosen as the "leader" too often. They might wonder why they never get a turn to lead. This can cause them to pull away from the group or try to disrupt the game so no one else can enjoy it. Grown-ups can help by guiding play in a way that gives each child a chance to feel included and valued.

Talking About Feelings

Children in their early years are still discovering the world of feelings. They might understand basic labels like "happy," "sad," or "angry," but "jealous" is more complicated. Parents and caregivers can help children by teaching them names for a wide range of emotions and talking about how those emotions appear in the body. For example, a child might say their tummy feels weird or their face feels hot. Connecting these physical sensations to the word "jealousy" can give the child a way to talk about what is happening inside them.

Storytelling is a useful tool here. Reading books or telling short tales about characters who feel jealous can help children see that the emotion is normal. They can watch how the characters handle it—whether they talk it out, find a way to share, or say sorry. After the story, asking the child simple questions like, "Why did that character get upset?" or "What could they do differently next time?" can gently guide them to think about their own lives.

Another helpful step is reassuring children that feeling jealous does not make them "bad." Young minds often see emotions as either good or bad. If they think jealousy is a "bad" emotion, they might deny or hide it, which can make the feeling grow. Showing understanding—saying things like, "It is okay to feel that way sometimes"—helps the child accept that jealousy is just another emotion they can learn to manage.

Handling Jealousy Among Peers

Children often form peer groups at school or in the neighborhood. They might compete over who can run the fastest, who can draw the best picture, or who has the newest toys. This environment can spark plenty of jealousy, especially if one child stands out. A child might become upset when a classmate is always the teacher's "helper," while they never get picked.

Grown-ups can help by encouraging kids to notice their own progress rather than constantly comparing themselves to others. For instance, a teacher might say, "Look at how much better you got at writing your name," rather than "You should write as neatly as your friend." When children focus on their own growth, they might feel less pressure to outdo someone else.

It is also helpful for kids to see that each person has different areas of strength. One child might be fast in running, another might be good at solving puzzles, another at painting. By spotlighting different talents, grown-ups can reduce the sense that only one skill or one child deserves all the praise. This can lower jealousy among peers and create a friendlier atmosphere.

The Role of Grown-Ups

Parents, teachers, grandparents, and others in a child's life can shape how kids handle jealousy. If grown-ups compare children openly—"Why can't you be more like your sister?"—the child might develop deeper jealous feelings. They may believe they are not as valued. On the flip side, if grown-ups give praise fairly, notice each child's special qualities, and avoid showing clear favorites, children are less likely to think they need to fight for attention.

Sometimes, grown-ups can unintentionally spark jealousy by going overboard with praise for one child's talents. It is good to recognize a child's achievements, but if the praise is always directed at the same child, siblings or classmates might feel overshadowed. Balancing praise is not about giving everyone the same number of compliments, but about noticing and encouraging each child's progress or effort. This approach helps each child feel seen.

When jealousy does show up, grown-ups can guide children to express their feelings in words. For example, if a child yells at a sibling, the parent might say, "Are you feeling upset because you think they got more attention?" This helps the child connect their actions to the underlying emotion. Once the feeling is identified, the parent can help the child find a better way to handle it—talking, sharing, or negotiating a fair turn.

Building Self-Worth in Childhood

A common source of jealousy is feeling that you are not good enough. If children grow up thinking they lack worth, they can be more sensitive when they see someone else doing well. They might worry that others are better liked or are better at everything. Helping children build a sense of self-worth can reduce the power of jealousy.

Self-worth in childhood can grow through tasks that allow kids to practice skills and see improvement. Simple activities like learning to tie shoelaces or riding a bike can show a child that they can achieve goals with practice. If a child hears, "You worked so hard and now you can do it on your own," they learn to value their own ability rather than comparing themselves to someone else.

Another part of building self-worth is teaching children that mistakes are okay. A child who believes any error means they are not good enough might become very jealous when others succeed. They could see another person's success as a reminder of their own failures. But if they learn that everyone makes mistakes and that mistakes can help us improve, they might be happier to let others have their moments of success without feeling overshadowed.

Step-Families and Blended Homes

When two families merge, children may suddenly have to share a parent with new siblings. They might also move into a new house or see a parent spending time with a step-parent. All of this can shake a child's sense of security, leading to jealous thoughts such as, "My dad is paying more attention to his new wife's children than to me," or "My mom has less time for me now."

It takes time for a blended family to find a comfortable rhythm. Children might test the new family members to see if they will be treated fairly. Step-siblings might compete for attention. Grown-ups in the home can help by having clear rules about how everyone is treated. They can set aside one-on-one time with each child so that no one feels left out. Being patient is important, as children might hold onto their jealousy until they feel fully accepted.

Talking about these feelings is key. Parents can ask children directly how they feel about the changes. This does not mean letting children run the house, but letting them share their fears can ease jealousy. Over time, if children see that all sides are respected, they are more likely to feel comfortable and let go of the idea that they must fight for attention.

Teaching Problem-Solving

When jealousy flares up, children often respond by crying, yelling, or taking things into their own hands. But they can learn healthier ways to respond if grown-ups show them how to solve problems calmly. For instance, if a child is jealous because a sibling gets a toy first, a parent can help them work out a plan: "Let your sibling have it for five minutes, and then it is your turn." Over time, children learn to suggest these solutions on their own.

Problem-solving might also include teaching children to ask for what they need. If a child feels jealous of a friend's new bike, they might say something mean out of envy. Instead, they could ask, "Could I try your bike for a minute?" or talk to a grown-up about earning or saving for a bike of their own. When children realize they have ways to address the root cause of their feelings, they might not go straight to jealous outbursts.

Learning Empathy

Empathy means understanding and sharing another person's feelings. If children can learn to imagine how others feel, they may be less likely to give in to jealous thoughts. For example, if a child thinks, "My friend is always better at drawing than me," they can also think, "Maybe my friend feels nervous about something else." This switch in perspective can show them that everyone has worries, and it might lessen their own envy.

Games and stories can build empathy. A teacher can ask children questions such as, "How would you feel if that happened to you?" or, "What do you think she is feeling right now?" By building this habit of thinking about others, children can see that they are not alone in having strong emotions. They begin to see the bigger picture, where each person has challenges and strengths. This can reduce the sense of competition that fuels jealousy.

Special Events and Comparisons

Early years often have special events—birthdays, holidays, school events—where attention might focus on one child more than another. During a sibling's birthday, for instance, the child who is not being celebrated might feel jealous because all eyes are on the birthday kid. They might wonder why they are not getting gifts or praise. Even if they understand the reason, their emotions might still flare up.

Grown-ups can prepare for this by talking ahead of time about what will happen and reminding the other child that their special day will come too. They might plan a small role for the sibling, like helping pass out treats, so they do not feel invisible. While the main spotlight is on the birthday child, including the sibling in a small but meaningful way can help them manage those feelings of being left out.

School events can also trigger jealousy. A child might not get picked for a part in the class performance or might not receive a prize at an awards ceremony. Parents and teachers can focus on praising the effort the child put in, rather than the result they received. They can also highlight how many ways there are to shine, so the child does not link self-worth only to the event that passed them by.

Preventing Harmful Comparisons

Adults sometimes compare children without meaning to do any harm. They might say, "Your sister is so neat with her handwriting," or "Your brother at your age was already riding a bike." Even if meant as encouragement, it can leave the child feeling they must match that sibling. This can lead to jealousy and resentment. Instead, adults can compare a child to their own past self, like saying, "Look how much better your handwriting is now compared to last month!"

Preventing harmful comparisons also involves celebrating different interests. If one child loves music and another loves drawing, they do not have to be judged on the same scale. Each child can be noticed for their own style and interests. This approach lowers the chance of them feeling jealous because they see that grown-ups appreciate the variety of talents in the family or classroom.

Warning Signs of Growing Jealousy

Sometimes, childhood jealousy can grow into bigger problems if not handled early. A child might start bullying a sibling or classmate, destroying others' things, or refusing to take part in family activities. They might show constant anger or sadness. If you see these signs, it might mean the child feels deeply insecure and needs more support.

Talking to a counselor, teacher, or pediatrician can help. These professionals might offer tips tailored to the child's situation. Early help can prevent jealous thoughts from turning into long-lasting bitterness or low self-esteem. Grown-ups should keep an open mind, because each child's reason for jealousy might be unique to their life experience and feelings.

Growing Through Jealousy

Even though jealousy can be tough, early childhood is also a time of quick learning. Children can learn to share, to express feelings with words, to solve problems peacefully, and to value their own progress. They might start out crying whenever a sibling gets attention, but with practice and guidance, they can learn to handle that moment calmly. They might even feel happy for their sibling once they feel secure in their own worth.

As children get older, they can look back and remember how they overcame their jealous moments. This can give them confidence in dealing with other challenges. They might realize that learning to talk about feelings and to share items or time helped them form better friendships. They can carry these lessons into later years, where jealousy might still appear in more complex situations, but they will have skills to manage it.

Conclusion

Jealousy in early years shows up in many ways: a child might push away a new sibling, refuse to share, or cry when a friend plays with someone else. While these behaviors can be frustrating for grown-ups, they are part of a child's effort to understand their place in the world. Children are learning what it means to have someone or something special and what happens when that special thing seems threatened.

Families, schools, and communities can ease childhood jealousy by teaching sharing and turn-taking, praising effort instead of just results, and helping children name and talk about their feelings. Adults can remember that children do not have the same ability to control impulses as older individuals do. Patience and calm explanations can go a long way. When children see that their feelings matter and that there are healthier ways to respond, they begin to trust the relationships around them.

Even though jealousy can cause tears and fights, it can also be a stepping stone in a child's emotional development. By guiding children to handle these moments with honesty and kindness, grown-ups help them gain skills that will benefit them for a lifetime. When children learn that they do not need to cling tightly to love, attention, or items, they may become more open-hearted and confident individuals, ready to connect with others without constant worry of being left out.

Through steady support and understanding, children can discover that they are important and valued, regardless of what others are doing. That assurance can lessen the sting of jealousy, freeing them to enjoy their early years with more peace and happiness.

Chapter 7: Jealousy in Romance

Romantic jealousy has a unique power. When you really like someone or share a life with them, the bond can feel strong and important. But because that bond matters so much, there can be worries about losing it. These worries can turn into jealousy. In this chapter, we will look at why romantic jealousy can be so intense, what might cause it, how it shows up in relationships, and ways people try to handle it.

The Bond That Feels Special

When two people care for each other in a romantic way, they often invest time, energy, and feelings into that bond. There might be shared plans and promises. The closeness can make a person feel safe. At the same time, it can also spark fear. A person might think, "What if my partner stops caring for me? What if they become close with someone else?" These questions tap into our wish to feel secure.

Romantic bonds can include physical closeness like hugging and holding hands, or they might simply be emotional closeness, such as long talks and inside jokes. Because these moments feel special, many people fear a third person stepping in. They worry that the partner might share these same moments with someone else. Even the thought of that can lead to jealous feelings.

The Roots of Romantic Jealousy

Romantic jealousy can stem from different places. One source is a fear of not being good enough. If a person has low confidence, they might think, "Maybe my partner will find someone better." Another source is past hurts. If someone was once left by a past partner, they might be on high alert with a new partner. They could imagine signs of betrayal where none exist.

Social ideas also play a part. In many cultures, people believe a partner should give all of their attention to just one person. If someone sees their partner texting a friend late at night, they might imagine hidden secrets. The fear often grows in the mind before any actual betrayal is proven. In some cases, the worry might be fair. But in many cases, it may be only a sign of deeper insecurities.

Worrying About Losing Love

Romantic jealousy often springs from the fear of losing someone we love. This fear can be powerful. In some situations, it leads a person to check a partner's phone or social media, or to ask endless questions. These acts might feel like they keep the relationship safe, but they can also push the partner away. No one likes feeling watched or distrusted for no reason.

Sometimes, the worry is not about actual facts but about imagined scenes. A person might picture their partner meeting a more interesting person at a party, sharing deep talks, and then drifting away from them. They might feel their stomach tighten, or their mind race, as if these scenes are real. This can lead to tension and stress that the partner does not understand. While it is normal to care about keeping a bond strong, it becomes a problem when we no longer see the difference between real threats and our own fears.

Signs of Romantic Jealousy

1. **Frequent Checking:** A person might look at a partner's social media or messages often, trying to see if anything suspicious appears.
2. **Endless Questions:** They might ask the same questions again and again: "Who were you with? What did you talk about? Why did it take so long?"
3. **Comparisons to Others:** The jealous person might compare themselves to anyone who talks to their partner, worrying that the other person is more fun or more attractive.
4. **Feeling Angry or Hurt:** The jealous partner might go from calm to upset quickly if they think the partner is giving attention to someone else.
5. **Pulling Away in Sadness:** Sometimes, jealousy does not cause anger but causes a person to withdraw, thinking, "I cannot trust you, so I will stop trying."

All of these signs reflect the same fear: that the person's place in the relationship is not secure.

Social Media and Romantic Jealousy

Technology makes it easier than ever to see who our partners talk to and what they "like" or comment on. A small action, like liking a photo, can bring up big doubts. A person might think, "Why did they like that person's photo? Are they attracted to them?" They might read too deeply into every small online gesture. This can create conflicts that are hard to solve because the proof is often uncertain. One person might say, "I was just being friendly," while the other believes, "You must be hiding something."

Some couples decide to limit how they use social media to avoid fights. Others agree on boundaries, like not following past crushes. But these measures only help if both partners trust each other and communicate. If jealousy runs high, even these steps might not calm the fear. The key is honest talk about online behavior and understanding each other's concerns without seeing them as silly.

Healthy vs. Unhealthy Jealousy

It might seem strange, but there can be a small side of jealousy that acts as a sign of caring. If it is mild and leads to open talk, it might help a couple notice their bond. For example, if one partner feels a pang of jealousy and says, "I realized I miss our time together," it can lead to plans to reconnect. This is different from extreme jealousy that leads to fights or restrictions. A small amount of jealousy might make people appreciate each other more.

Unhealthy jealousy is marked by suspicion that does not go away, trying to control a partner, or seeing all interactions as threats. It can lead to constant stress in a relationship and might even cause emotional or verbal harm. In such cases, it is crucial to see that jealousy has gone too far. Both partners might need help, such as talking to a counselor, learning new ways to talk, or building self-esteem.

Communication Matters

One of the best ways to handle romantic jealousy is open and calm communication. If you feel uneasy, telling your partner directly can help more than staying silent or snooping. For example, you might say, "I feel worried when you spend a lot of time texting that friend. Can we talk about what that means?" This starts a conversation based on honesty rather than blame. The partner can then explain the nature of the friendship, easing your mind.

However, good communication means both sides must be willing to listen. If one partner shuts down the talk by saying, "You are just being silly," the jealous partner might feel even more worried. A better response could be, "I see you are upset. Let me explain why this should not worry you." This approach respects the fear, even if the fear is based on mistaken ideas.

Trust as the Core of Romance

At the center of romantic bonds is trust. Trust means believing that the other person cares for you and will keep your bond safe. When trust is strong, a person can handle small doubts without spiraling. If their partner talks to someone else, they assume it is friendly, not a sign of betrayal. If their partner comes home late, they accept that traffic or an extra errand was the cause, not a secret meeting.

Building trust takes time. Each honest action builds it a bit stronger. Each moment of kindness or loyalty tells the other person, "I care for you; you matter to me." When trust is damaged, jealousy can rush in. Mending trust might involve apologies, changed actions, or therapy if the hurt is deep. But when trust is restored, jealousy often loses some of its hold.

Past Experiences and Fear

People sometimes bring past wounds into a new relationship. If they were cheated on before, they might become extra wary. They might check for small clues that the same thing could happen again. It is natural to want to protect ourselves, but this can hurt a new bond if we treat a trustworthy partner like they are guilty before any real evidence appears.

Partners can help by showing patience and proving with actions that they are loyal. But the person with past hurts might also need to work on healing. That can mean talking to someone they trust, writing down their worries, or reminding themselves, "This is a new person, and I will not treat them as if they have already hurt me." Over time, these steps can lessen the fear.

When Jealousy Becomes Control

There is a difference between expressing jealousy and trying to control a partner's life. Some people might want to know exactly where their partner is at all times, demand constant updates, or refuse to let them see friends. This crosses a line into controlling behavior. It often comes from deep insecurity, but it can be harmful and is not a sign of true care.

If you or someone you know is in a situation where one partner controls the other due to jealousy, it is important to get help. A healthy relationship allows both partners to have freedom and trust. It does not mean ignoring each other's needs, but it does mean each person can have friends, hobbies, and a life outside the relationship without fear of punishment.

The Danger of Silent Jealousy

Not everyone who feels jealous shows it loudly. Some keep it inside, pretending everything is fine. Over time, this jealousy might build up, causing silent resentment. A person might say they do not mind something, but inside they feel hurt or betrayed. This can slowly eat away at the affection in a relationship.

Silent jealousy can show up in subtle actions: a partner might act distant, give short replies, or make snippy remarks. The other partner might be confused about what is going on. Honest talk can break this pattern. Saying, "I need to tell you how I really feel," can open the door to fix misunderstandings before they grow large.

Comparing Romantic Partners

Sometimes, jealousy emerges when a person compares their own relationship to others. They might think, "Our friends are so happy. Why are we not like that?"

or "My partner used to be more caring—maybe they treat someone else that way now." These thoughts can breed jealousy of a past version of the partner or of another couple's bond. But such comparisons are often unfair. We do not see what goes on in private for other couples, and relationships change over time.

Focusing on what is within your own connection can help. Talking about what you each want now and how you both can feel valued is more useful than wondering if your partner wishes they were with someone else. By putting energy into the real relationship rather than imagined ones, couples can keep jealousy from growing.

Common Myths About Romantic Jealousy

- **Myth 1: If You Love Someone, You Should Feel Jealous.**
  Some people think that jealousy is proof of deep care. But too much jealousy can be a sign of insecurity, not love. Love can show itself in trust, respect, and kindness rather than constant worry.
- **Myth 2: A Partner Should Never Talk to Anyone Else.**
  It is unrealistic to expect a partner to never talk or be friendly with others. Friendships and connections outside the couple are normal. The key is respecting the bond and having healthy boundaries.
- **Myth 3: Jealousy Means the Partner Did Something Wrong.**
  Sometimes, jealousy comes from our own fears or misunderstandings rather than the partner's actual behavior. It is important to look at facts before blaming someone for causing jealousy.

Dealing with Romantic Jealousy Day by Day

1. **Notice Triggers**: Pay attention to what sparks your jealousy. Is it a text message from a certain friend? Is it seeing your partner talk to someone attractive? Recognizing the trigger can help you think more clearly about it.
2. **Pause Before Reacting**: If you feel jealousy rising, take a moment to breathe. This gives you time to check if your fears are real or just assumptions.

3. **Use Calm Words**: Instead of accusing, start with how you feel: "I felt worried when I saw you talking so closely with them. Can you tell me what was going on?" This invites a response rather than starting a fight.
4. **Build Self-Worth**: Remind yourself of your own strengths and positive traits. If you believe in your own value, you may not fear losing your partner as much.
5. **Share Concerns**: Talk openly with your partner about your worries without making them feel guilty right away. Give them a chance to assure you or explain.
6. **Seek Help If Needed**: If jealousy leads to big arguments or controlling actions, a counselor or trusted advisor might help you both work through deeper issues.

Keeping the Spark Without the Fear

Some couples wonder how to keep their close bond and sense of safety without letting jealousy take over. One approach is to remind each other often of what makes the relationship important. Little notes, kind words, or planned time together can help reassure both partners. This reassurance can reduce the urge to seek proof that the bond is still strong.

Another approach is to respect each other's need for personal space. Spending time with friends, enjoying hobbies, or visiting family alone does not have to threaten the relationship. In fact, it can keep each person healthy and happy, which can make the bond better. When people trust each other to have some independence, there is less to be jealous about.

Growing Together

Over time, if two people learn to handle jealousy in small, honest ways, they might grow closer. They see that they can face challenges together rather than against each other. They learn that talking openly about worries can prevent bigger rifts later. This growth can make them feel more confident in themselves and in their connection.

On the other hand, if jealousy is never addressed, it can pile up. A person might grow bitter, thinking, "They never respect my concerns," or, "I always have to defend myself." Over many months or years, this can drive two people apart. That is why spotting and handling jealousy early is so important. It saves the bond from damage.

The Role of Forgiveness

In some relationships, mistakes happen. Perhaps a partner truly overstepped boundaries, flirting too much or hiding messages. If the couple decides to stay together, the jealous partner might need to forgive. Forgiveness does not mean forgetting or saying it was okay, but it means choosing not to hold it over the other person forever. This can be hard, especially if trust was deeply shaken.

The partner who made the mistake must show real change to rebuild trust. They might offer to be more transparent, share details of their day, or be more open about their online accounts. Over time, these changes can show the jealous partner that the bond is safe again. Both sides must agree that they want to heal rather than keep reliving the mistake.

Long-Distance Relationships

Jealousy can be even stronger in long-distance bonds. When partners do not see each other often, it is easy to imagine what the other might be doing. A delayed reply to a message can cause panic. A post showing a partner out with friends can set off worries about their faithfulness.

In these cases, setting clear ways to stay in touch helps. Video calls, voice notes, and shared updates can ease doubts. Having plans for the next visit can also create a sense of security. Both partners must trust that the time apart does not mean their love is fading. If they cannot hold onto that trust, jealousy might grow unchecked.

Romantic Jealousy Across Different Ages

Young couples, like teenagers, might feel jealousy in strong waves because they are new to romance. They may not have practiced coping skills yet. They might compare themselves to peers or panic if their partner even talks to someone else. With time, they can learn healthier ways to handle these fears.

Older couples, too, can face jealousy. Life changes—like a new job, meeting new people, or health challenges—can make one partner feel insecure. This can reignite old worries. But older couples might also draw on the trust they have built. They have more memories and shared experiences to remind them of their bond. This can help them calm those jealous thoughts.

Conclusion

Romantic jealousy can be one of the strongest forms of jealousy because it touches the deep part of us that wants to be loved and wanted. It comes from fears about losing a precious bond, from past hurts, or from social pressure. The signs can range from mild worry to extreme control. Communication and trust are the main tools for handling jealousy in a healthy way.

Each couple will face some kind of jealous moment at some point. How they handle it can either bring them closer or drive them apart. By talking calmly, respecting each other's space, building self-worth, and working on trust, people can keep jealousy in check. Though it might never vanish fully, it can remain small enough that it does not damage the love they share.

Chapter 8: Jealousy in Families

Families are among the closest groups people belong to, whether that means parents and children, siblings, or extended relatives like aunts, uncles, and grandparents. Because family bonds can be so strong, jealousy in this setting can feel especially hurtful. It can affect many aspects of daily life. In this chapter, we look at different ways jealousy appears in families, what triggers it, and how family members can handle it in kinder ways.

Different Kinds of Family Bonds

Families can look very different. Some include a mother, father, and children. Others have single parents, two mothers, or two fathers. Still others include grandparents, cousins, and close family friends. No matter the shape of a family, many people within it might share a home or spend a lot of time together. They see each other on both good days and bad days.

In these close quarters, many issues can develop. People can compete for attention, help, or even just quiet time. When jealousy appears, it may affect one person first, but soon it can involve the entire household. For example, a child might get jealous of a sibling, leading parents to step in. This can create stress for everyone. Recognizing how jealousy starts is the first step to making the family calmer.

Jealousy Between Parents

Many people think jealousy only appears between siblings or between children and parents. But parents themselves can feel jealous in certain situations. One parent might be jealous of the time the other parent spends with the kids. They might worry that the kids like the other parent more. Or they might be jealous of a partner's success outside the home, thinking, "They get praise at work while I get none here."

Parents can also feel a twinge of jealousy if a child shows more respect or love toward the other parent. This might be especially true in blended families, where a child bonds quickly with a step-parent. The biological parent might worry that their own connection to the child is fading. These feelings can be strong, yet parents might not admit them, fearing it sounds childish to be jealous of their own partner or child.

Jealousy Toward a Parent's New Partner

When a parent starts a new relationship—perhaps after a divorce or loss—children can feel jealous of the newcomer. They might see the new person as taking the parent's time or attention. Teenagers might be especially sensitive to this, worrying that they will have less say in family matters. They may compare the new partner to the parent they remember or to a past step-parent who caused pain.

In such cases, children often need reassurance that they are not being replaced. The parent can spend one-on-one time with them and show that their bond is still strong. The new partner can also be mindful not to force themselves into the child's life too quickly. Moving at a steady pace can help ease the child's jealousy. Over time, respect and kindness might lead to a better relationship for everyone involved.

Sibling Rivalry

One of the most common forms of family jealousy is sibling rivalry. Siblings share parents and a home, so they notice every difference in how they are treated. If one child seems to get more praise or more freedom, the other might feel jealous. They might lash out, argue, or try to prove they are better.

For instance, an older sibling might feel jealous of a younger one who gets away with mistakes. They might think, "Mom never let me do that when I was younger!" Or a younger sibling might feel jealous because the older one is allowed to stay out later. These normal differences in rules, shaped by age or maturity, can still spark jealous thoughts in a child who does not see the bigger picture.

Parents can reduce sibling jealousy by explaining the reasoning behind certain rules or privileges. They might say, "Your brother is older, so he can handle a later bedtime. When you reach his age, you can too." Fairness is important, but it does not always mean doing exactly the same thing for every child. Clear explanations can help children feel that decisions are not random or favoring one child for no reason.

Grandparents and Their Favorite Grandkids

Sometimes, grandparents can unintentionally set off jealousy by having favorites. They might shower one grandchild with gifts or praise, making the others feel overlooked. This can cause confusion. The grandchild who does not get special attention might think, "What am I doing wrong?" This can lead to jealousy not only toward the grandchild who is favored but also toward the grandparent for seeming unfair.

Families can address this gently by talking openly. If a parent sees that their child is hurt by a grandparent's actions, they can pull the grandparent aside and explain. Often, grandparents do not realize the effect of their behavior. Maybe they relate more to one grandchild's hobby or see that child more often. With a little awareness, they can balance their attention among the grandchildren.

Adult Sibling Jealousy

Jealousy does not always vanish when siblings grow up. Adult siblings can still feel jealousy over careers, houses, or their parents' attention. One sibling might earn more money or have a larger home, leading the other to feel jealous of their success. The success might remind them of their own struggles.

Parent care can also spark conflict among adult siblings. For example, if an elderly parent depends on one child for help, that child might feel stressed. Meanwhile, the other siblings might be jealous if they believe the parent favors the caregiver. Or they might feel relieved they are not the ones helping, which could cause tension. These issues are complex because they tie into old family dynamics that go back decades.

Communication can be tricky here, but it is key. Adult siblings can hold family meetings to discuss responsibilities and how their parents' needs will be handled. If they see jealousy rising, they can name it: "I feel left out because Dad always calls you first." Bringing these feelings into the open can help avoid bottled-up resentment.

Competition for Parents' Approval

Children of any age can crave their parents' approval. A child might think, "If I score the winning goal, Dad will like me more." This can lead to fierce competition between siblings, each trying to show they are the best. When parents give one child more nods or positive words, the other might become jealous. In some cases, the child may stop trying altogether, thinking, "I can never beat them, so why bother?"

It helps when parents notice effort rather than just outcomes. Instead of praising the child who gets the best grades or wins the most awards, parents can praise each child for trying their best. They can also avoid direct comparisons. Saying, "Why can't you be more like your sister?" can harm a child's self-esteem and create deeper jealousy. Instead, focusing on each child's progress can build a sense of personal pride rather than a race for parent approval.

In-Law Dynamics

When people get married, new family relationships form. In-laws can sometimes feel jealous if they think their child's spouse takes too much time away. A mother might say, "You used to visit every weekend, but now you spend all your time with your partner's family." The spouse might feel jealous of the closeness between their partner and the partner's parent. These jealousies can lead to tense meals and awkward visits if not handled.

Clear boundaries help. A couple can decide how often they will visit each side of the family. They can talk openly with their parents, saying, "We love you, but we also have to make decisions that work for us." Balancing traditions from both sides can help reduce jealousy. If in-laws see they are not being ignored, they might accept the new ways of spending time.

Caring for Aging Family Members

As relatives get older, caring for them can become a main issue in the family. Siblings might fight over who does the most work or who has the final say in decisions about a parent's health. This can cause jealousy if one sibling feels overburdened while another sibling appears to do less. Or the one doing less might be jealous of the sibling who is closer to the parent, even if that closeness comes with heavy responsibilities.

Talking as a group about how to share tasks can help. Some siblings might provide money, while others give time. There could also be a rotation of visits. By matching each person's strengths and limits, families can spread out the tasks in a fair way. This approach might prevent the feeling that one person carries all the weight while others stand by.

Family Events and Gatherings

Holidays, birthdays, and other gatherings can be special times for families, but they can also bring out hidden jealousies. Perhaps one branch of the family arrives with expensive gifts, making another branch feel less successful. Or a cousin might talk about their recent achievements, and others feel jealous for not having such news to share. Even meal preferences can lead to conflict if one person's favorite dish always gets made, while another's never does.

Planning these gatherings with care can help lessen jealous feelings. Family members might agree to keep gifts simple or focus more on the company rather than what each person brings. They can also allow each family member to pick a favorite dish, ensuring everyone feels included. These small acts of consideration can keep jealousy from ruining what could be a pleasant time.

Handling Blended Families

Blended families, where children and step-parents share a home, often deal with complicated forms of jealousy. A child might feel loyal to their biological mother or father and resent the new step-parent. Or step-siblings might compare how they are treated, thinking the parent or step-parent favors their own children.

Some children feel torn, wanting a good relationship with the step-parent but worrying that it will upset their biological parent.

Respecting each child's comfort level is important. A step-parent does not have to rush into a full parent role. They can build trust slowly, by listening and being supportive. The biological parent can help by reassuring the child, "I will always be your parent. That will not change." Over time, new bonds can form if the family members give each other space to adjust. Jealousy might still appear in small ways, but calm talks can address it before it grows.

Finances and Property

Money can cause jealousy within families, especially if some members earn more or inherit property. A sibling might look at another's wealth and think, "They never have to worry about bills; it's not fair." Or parents might favor one child in their will, causing the others to feel cheated. These issues can stir up old grudges and spark big fights.

Open and fair discussions about money might help. If parents plan to pass on property, talking with the family in advance can clear the air. It does not mean everyone will be perfectly happy, but they will not be shocked. For siblings who compare incomes, it can help to remember that each person's path is different. Rather than building jealousy, they could share advice and support, turning the family into a resource rather than a battlefield.

The Cost of Hidden Jealousy

In some families, jealousy is never discussed. It stays under the surface as silent resentment. A sister might always feel the parents liked her brother more. A grown child might think a parent admires another sibling's achievements more. This unspoken jealousy can poison relationships, causing people to act distant, speak in an unfriendly tone, or avoid family gatherings.

Bringing jealousy out into the open can be scary, but it might free everyone from years of tension. A person could say, "I have felt for a long time that you prefer Sam over me. Is that true?" Another could respond, "I had no idea you felt that way. Let's talk about it." While these talks can be uncomfortable, they can also lead to better understanding. Even if some of the jealousy remains, knowing it is recognized can lessen its power.

Teaching Children About Fairness and Kindness

A big part of preventing family jealousy involves teaching children from a young age that each person in the family is valued. Parents can show that fairness does not always mean the same treatment for all, but rather giving each person what they need. For example, a teenager might need money for a school trip, while a younger child might need more direct supervision. Both children are getting what helps them most at their age.

When children see that parents are consistent in their rules and do not play favorites, they learn trust. They realize that if another sibling seems to get something special, it might just be their turn for that moment. Talking through these rules and decisions can build understanding. Children might still feel jealous at times, but they will have the tools to handle it in a calmer way.

Balancing Family Roles

Some family members take on strong roles, such as the problem-solver, the peacekeeper, or the high achiever. Others might feel jealous if they think only one person gets praise or respect. A sister might say, "He is always the one people go to for advice. I guess I am not smart enough." This can lead to bitterness. But families can share roles more evenly.

Encouraging each person to speak up, help out, or show their own strength can prevent one person from doing everything. If big decisions are made by only one family member, others might never gain the confidence to contribute. By inviting each person to share opinions or ideas, families can spread tasks around. This helps each member feel respected, lowering jealous feelings.

Creating a Supportive Atmosphere

Families can choose to handle jealousy by fostering an atmosphere of support. This means praising each other's progress, lending a hand in hard times, and talking honestly about problems. In such a family, if a child feels jealous of a sibling's skill, the parents might say, "Why not ask them to teach you?" or "Let's see what you are good at, too."

Some families hold regular chats where everyone can share something they achieved or something they are excited about. This can remind members that each person has a place. Jealousy often arises when someone thinks, "I do not matter as much." By highlighting each person's good points, the family reduces that worry.

Handling Jealousy in Extended Families

Extended families might have a cousin who seems to be everyone's favorite. They might arrive at gatherings and get all the hugs, while others watch from the sidelines. This can cause jealousy between cousins or among siblings. If the adults notice this, they can make a point of greeting everyone warmly, not just the cousin with the biggest personality.

Other times, an aunt or uncle might feel jealous if grandparents spend more time at one sibling's home. They might think, "You never visit us." Rather than letting that build, they can extend an invitation or suggest rotating visits. Clear plans can fix misunderstandings. Maybe the grandparents stayed with one sibling because it was closer to a hospital they needed. By sharing facts, the jealous feelings can calm.

Step by Step Toward a Healthier Family

1. **Notice the Signs**: Watch for clues that someone is feeling jealous, like sulking, speaking sharply, or withdrawing.
2. **Open Dialogue**: Gently ask questions to see if jealousy is at the root of the issue: "I sense you are upset. Do you feel overlooked?"

3. **Find Fair Solutions**: Talk about each person's needs. Brainstorm ways to spread attention and responsibilities.
4. **Respect Limits**: Each person has a right to their feelings, but not a right to harm others. If jealousy leads to insults or aggression, the family must address it right away.
5. **Offer Reassurance**: Sometimes, family members just need a reminder that they are loved. A kind word or a thoughtful act can ease jealousy.
6. **Seek Outside Help If Needed**: If jealousy causes ongoing arguments, therapy or talking with a counselor can help the family untangle deeper problems.

Conclusion

Jealousy in families is often rooted in the wish to feel valued and secure. Children can feel jealous of siblings, parents can feel jealous of each other, and extended relatives can become upset over differences in attention or success. The close bonds in a family mean that each person's actions can affect everyone else.

By spotting the signs early and talking about them, families can handle jealousy before it grows too large. Clear rules, balanced praise, and open sharing can build trust. While no family is perfect, efforts to address jealousy can make home life calmer and more caring. When each member feels accepted for who they are, jealousy loses much of its power. Then the family can focus on supporting each other, learning, and growing in their own ways, free from constant worry about who is getting more or less.

Chapter 9: Jealousy in Different Cultures

Jealousy is a common emotion around the world, but it is not always viewed or handled in the same way. Different cultures have their own beliefs, customs, and ways of interacting that can shape how jealousy looks and how people respond to it. In this chapter, we will explore how jealousy can be seen and managed in various parts of the globe. We will also look at what these differences tell us about the human need to feel valued and secure.

Cultural Views of Emotions

In some places, people freely show how they feel. They might laugh when they are happy, cry when they are sad, and talk loudly when they are angry. These cultures might expect jealousy to be expressed openly. If a person feels jealous, they might say so plainly or show it through facial expressions and gestures. Others around them might accept this as normal, offering advice or calming words.

In other cultures, it might be polite to hide strong feelings. A person who feels jealous might try not to show it, because displaying such emotions is viewed as awkward or improper. They might smile while feeling upset inside. In these places, family or friends might guess that someone is jealous, but they could think it is rude to bring it up directly. This difference in emotional display means that jealousy might be dealt with in quieter, more private ways.

There is no single "right" or "wrong" way to handle jealousy across cultures. Each group has its history and customs that lead to certain norms. Still, these norms can shape how often jealousy comes up, how strong it gets, and whether people share it openly or keep it hidden. In a culture that encourages open talk, jealousy might be resolved quickly but also might spark arguments if people do not watch their tone. In a culture that discourages open talk, jealousy might remain hidden for a long time, leading to silent resentment.

Romantic Relationships and Social Expectations

One major area where jealousy shows up is in romantic bonds. Different cultures have various beliefs about dating, marriage, and loyalty. In some regions, people expect a couple to spend most of their free time together. If one partner hangs out with friends too often, the other might feel jealous and say, "You should be with me instead." This can lead to strict rules about what is acceptable for a partner to do.

Other cultures might encourage couples to spend time apart with friends or have more flexible boundaries. If a person grows up in such a setting, they might not see a partner's independent social life as a threat. They may think it is natural for each person to have personal hobbies and friendships. Jealousy may still arise, but it might be less intense because people are used to this kind of freedom.

In some communities, arranged marriages are common. A couple may be brought together by their families rather than through their own choice. At times, one or both people might feel jealous if they fear they cannot form a strong bond with their partner. They might also worry if their partner shows friendliness toward someone else, not knowing if that could blossom into something deeper. Alternatively, in places where arranged marriages are the norm, there might be clear guidelines about what is and is not allowed, which can limit the chance for jealousy—at least publicly.

Polygamy and Group Marriages

In some parts of the world, there are cultures that allow or encourage having more than one spouse. This can be seen in forms of polygamy, where one man may have multiple wives or, in rarer cases, one woman may have several husbands. People outside these cultures might expect jealousy to be massive in such families. However, the reality can be complicated.

In polygamous communities, there are often social rules that help lessen jealousy. For example, a husband might divide his time equally among all wives. Each wife could have her own living area, and there might be set schedules for visits. These customs try to lower the feeling that one wife is favored over another. Still, jealousy can happen. Some wives might feel overlooked if they see another wife getting more attention or resources. Others might handle their worries quietly, talking to older relatives for advice on controlling jealous thoughts. In many cases, the group is aware of the risk of jealousy and works to limit it.

People who live in communities that practice polygamy might feel less alarmed by the idea of sharing a partner, because they grow up learning that such arrangements are normal. Yet, outside views might label these arrangements as unfair or bound to cause envy. This shows how culture shapes what we expect, how we deal with suspicion, and how we handle possible feelings of being replaced.

Extended Family and Group Life

In some cultures, big extended families share one home or live very close. Grandparents, aunts, uncles, and cousins might all be part of day-to-day life. Children might be cared for by many relatives, not just their parents. This communal approach can both ease and increase jealousy.

On the one hand, because many people share the tasks of raising children, a parent might feel relieved rather than jealous. They know their child is safe with close relatives. On the other hand, a mother or father could feel left out if a child grows attached to a grandparent or aunt, seeking them for comfort instead of the parent. The parent might think, "They like you more than me," which can spark jealous feelings.

For children, living in a large family might mean they have multiple adult figures providing support. But it can also lead them to compare the time and attention they receive with what other kids in the extended family get. If one child is seen as the "star" of the family—maybe they do well in school or excel at a sport—other children might feel jealous. Cultural expectations can either lessen this tension by reminding everyone that the family's success is shared, or they can make it worse if comparisons are encouraged.

Honor and Reputation

In certain societies, a family's honor or reputation is of high importance. If a person thinks a relative's behavior might harm the family's standing, they could become jealous or angry. For example, in places where a family's name must remain respected, a brother might feel jealous if his sister talks to men outside the family's social circle. He might fear that her actions could bring shame on the family. This type of jealousy is not simply about personal feelings but also about the social cost of losing face in the community.

Such worries can be powerful. People might feel pressure to monitor relatives to ensure they do not break the rules. This can lead to conflicts, because the relative being watched might feel smothered. At times, this watchfulness can go too far, becoming controlling or even harmful. In these extreme cases, jealousy is tied to larger social beliefs, making it more difficult to solve through calm conversations alone.

Workplace and Achievement Jealousy in Various Cultures

Jealousy does not only appear in family or romantic settings. It also shows up at work. Different cultures have different approaches to employment, achievement, and success. Some societies reward competition among workers. People might fight for promotions and raises, leading to envy if one person seems to always get ahead. Others might favor group success, encouraging workers to support each other. In that environment, someone's victory might be seen as good for the entire group, reducing jealousy.

In some places, respect for seniority or age is crucial. Younger workers might feel jealous if they are not allowed to rise quickly, even if they have fresh ideas or skills. They could see older coworkers receiving privileges just for being older. Conversely, older workers might feel jealous if a company suddenly favors youthful voices or new graduates. These feelings can affect how people work together.

Global companies that bring together people from many cultures might face a mix of attitudes. One person could view a coworker's promotion as well-deserved, while another sees it as an unfair act of favoritism. Managers might have to balance different expectations to keep the team united. This can be done by setting clear guidelines about how achievements are measured and rewarded, so employees do not feel one culture's norms override another's.

Social Media Across Cultures

Social media has reached almost every corner of the planet, but how people use it can differ by culture. In some areas, people post many photos of their daily lives, from meals to social events. In other places, people share fewer personal details. These habits can affect jealousy. Where many personal posts are common, someone might feel jealous seeing a friend's fancy trip or new house. In more reserved areas, people might become jealous over smaller details, such as a partner's single photo with a coworker.

Language differences can also cause misunderstandings. A friendly chat in one culture might be seen as flirting in another. Emojis or symbols might carry varied meanings, leading to confusion about the true intent of an online interaction. This confusion can spark jealousy if a person thinks their partner or friend is stepping over a boundary.

Because social media crosses borders, it can link people with different norms. Two people might date online and come from contrasting cultural backgrounds. Their ideas of what is okay to post or how much contact is acceptable with old friends can clash, leading to jealousy. For these long-distance or cross-cultural connections, open talk about expectations is key.

Religion and Belief Systems

Beliefs play a big part in how people handle emotions. Many religions teach guidelines on love, kindness, and self-control. Some might say jealousy is a harmful feeling to avoid, linking it to greed or pride. Others might accept a mild level of jealousy as normal but suggest believers keep it in check by thinking of others' needs. In communities where religious teachings shape daily life, people might use prayer or talk to a spiritual leader when they feel envy or suspicion.

Some faiths also shape family structure. There might be rules about men and women's roles or about how marriages should work. This can influence jealousy. If a culture's religious teachings say that men handle outside business and women run the home, a man might feel jealous or threatened if his wife starts a new career. A woman might feel jealous if she sees her husband interacting with female coworkers, especially if local customs disapprove of men and women mixing freely. These religious or cultural norms can greatly affect how a couple handles daily stresses.

Public vs. Private Jealousy

Another factor is whether jealousy is shown in public or kept private. In some cultures, public scenes are considered shameful, so arguments are kept behind closed doors. Families might deal with jealous rifts quietly, never letting neighbors or acquaintances see the problem. Outsiders might think everything is peaceful, even if tensions run high behind the scenes.

Elsewhere, people could be more open about disagreements, even in public. If a person sees someone flirting with their partner at a social event, they might speak up loudly right there. This might shock visitors from a culture where such conflicts are always private. However, in an open setting, the problem might be aired and resolved quickly rather than festering in silence. Each approach has its pros and cons. Public airing can lead to immediate solutions but might also cause embarrassment. Private handling can protect everyone's dignity but might also allow resentment to grow if not resolved.

Collectivist vs. Individualist Cultures

One idea researchers often note is the difference between collectivist and individualist cultures. In collectivist places, people focus on the group's well-being. A family or community might come before a single person's wants. Meanwhile, individualist cultures favor personal freedom and personal success. Neither style is better or worse overall, but they can affect how jealousy happens.

In a collectivist culture, a person might feel jealous if they believe a family member is bringing shame or trouble to the entire group. They might fear that this person's actions reflect poorly on them. Tensions can rise if the group believes the individual is ignoring their duty. On the flip side, jealousy might be less common about personal achievements, because sharing success is expected.

In an individualist culture, personal success can bring out jealousy more often. If one person does very well at school or work, others might feel envious of their progress. They see it as a reflection of the individual's worth. At the same time, people might be more accepting of the idea that each person has their own life, so jealousy that springs from family ties might be weaker. These broad strokes do not apply to every single person, but they offer insight into patterns seen worldwide.

Handling Jealousy Through Rituals and Customs

Some cultures have specific rituals or customs meant to prevent or reduce jealousy. For instance, in certain small communities, if a person receives a large gift or bounty, they might share it right away with neighbors to keep envy at bay. They believe that by sharing good fortune, they avoid stirring jealousy. This might include distributing meat from a successful hunt or giving part of a harvest to others. Such traditions help maintain social harmony.

Elsewhere, there may be events (small gatherings or discussions) where community members air their concerns or conflicts. People can speak openly about feeling envy or being wronged, and community elders might guide them to a resolution. In these cases, jealousy is treated as a common issue that can be fixed through shared wisdom. The idea is that by bringing jealousy into the open and finding fair outcomes, the group stays united.

Urban vs. Rural Settings

Differences between urban and rural lifestyles can also shape how jealousy appears. In a big city, people might have more freedom to choose friends, partners, and jobs. They might also face stronger competition, leading to envy if they see others moving up the ladder more quickly. In a rural area, people tend to know each other well, and traditions might be more fixed. The closeness can make jealousy deeper if someone feels everyone knows their private issues. At the same time, it can also mean that people are more willing to step in and help calm tensions.

For instance, in a small village, if a person starts to feel jealous of a neighbor's rising wealth, they might talk to a local leader or relative. Because the group is tight, others might notice the tension quickly and step in to keep the peace. In a large city, a person might not have the same tight-knit circle. They could feel alone in their envy, with fewer people stepping in to guide them. Both settings come with unique pluses and minuses when dealing with jealousy.

Cross-Cultural Friendships and Couples

As people travel or move to new places, cross-cultural friendships and couples become more common. These bonds can be very fulfilling, but they also bring challenges. Different ideas of what is polite, how much personal space is normal, or how men and women should act can all spark misunderstandings. For instance, if one partner is from a culture that values open discussion and the other from a culture that values silence, jealousy concerns might get lost in confusion. One person might ask many questions, thinking, "We should talk this out." The other might feel attacked and think, "Why are you making a scene?"

To handle jealousy in such relationships, both sides can learn about each other's backgrounds. This involves asking questions, being open to new perspectives, and not assuming a person is acting with bad intentions. If a friend or partner from another culture does something that seems suspicious, it might just be their normal way of socializing. Over time, with patience, cross-cultural pairs can find common ground that respects both traditions.

Keeping an Open Mind

Seeing how jealousy is viewed and handled in different places reminds us that our way is not the only way. For example, if we believe romantic partners must share all details of their day, we might be puzzled that some cultures think it is okay to keep certain friendships private. Or if we think families should speak out loud about every conflict, we might struggle to understand a household that deals with jealousies behind closed doors.

Learning about these differences can help us manage our own jealous feelings more calmly. We realize that many triggers for jealousy are shaped by how we were raised or by local beliefs. If we move or travel to a new place, we might see new ways of dealing with these feelings. We can learn from others, adopting ideas that help us feel more at ease. At the same time, we can share our own insights about direct communication or acceptance.

Conclusion

Jealousy may be universal, but it is not simple. Every culture adds its own spin, shaped by history, religion, social structures, and daily habits. In some places, jealousy is shouted from the rooftops. In others, it is hidden behind polite smiles. Some communities have routines that share wealth and success to avoid stirring envy, while others treat personal triumph as a private matter. Romantic relationships might be handled with strict guidelines in one culture and more loosely in another.

By looking at these differences, we see that jealousy is not just a personal feeling; it is shaped by the world around us. Culture can either make jealousy flare more easily or guide it toward calm solutions. When we learn about these views, we gain a wider understanding of how humans everywhere deal with the fear of losing what they hold dear. This knowledge can also help us be kinder and more flexible when jealousy shows up in our own relationships or in those of people from different backgrounds.

Understanding these cultural angles does not mean jealousy goes away, but it can help us see that no single approach fits everyone. Each society has found its own ways—some gentle, some stern—to manage this powerful emotion. By respecting these differences and learning from them, we can make progress in handling jealousy in a way that strengthens, rather than weakens, our connections with others.

Chapter 10: Jealousy in Animals

Many people think jealousy is only a human emotion, linked to our ability to imagine future events or dwell on the past. Yet, studies and observations suggest that various animals might also show jealousy-like behaviors. Whether it is a dog pushing another dog aside for a pat, or a monkey reacting angrily when food is shared unevenly, we see signs that animals sense unfairness and guard what they see as "theirs." In this chapter, we will explore examples of jealousy in different species, why it might have evolved, and what that teaches us about our own feelings.

Do Animals Really Feel Jealousy?

When we talk about animals feeling jealousy, we need to be careful. Animals cannot tell us in words, "I feel jealous." Instead, we watch their actions and see if they match what we recognize as jealousy. For example, if a pet dog becomes upset when its owner gives attention to another dog, we might see whining, barking, or trying to wedge itself between the owner and the other dog. This looks a lot like the dog is saying, "Hey, do not ignore me!"

Behavior experts note that while animals may not think about jealousy the same way people do, they can show protective or competitive actions that seem similar. They might guard a resource—like food, toys, or a caretaker's attention—if they sense it is at risk of being taken away. This guarding might include nudging the rival aside, whining, or even snapping. In social species, these reactions help the animal keep resources or bonds that are key for survival.

Jealousy in Dogs

Dogs are often the first animals that come to mind when talking about jealous behavior. Many dog owners say their pet gets upset if they pay attention to another dog. If the owner pets a new dog, their own dog might bark or try to climb into the owner's lap. Some dogs might even go as far as growling or snapping. Researchers have tried to test this by placing dogs in controlled settings. For instance, an owner might pet a stuffed dog or a toy that looks like an animal. The real dog often reacts with signs of aggression or tries to push the toy away.

Why would dogs act this way? Dogs are pack animals. In the wild, they have a group structure. Attention and loyalty matter for survival. If a dog sees the bond with its human as important, it might guard that bond from possible threats. It is not guaranteed that every dog acts jealous, but many do seem to show some version of protective behavior that we call jealousy.

Cats and Their Territorial Nature

Cats may seem less attached to people than dogs, but they too can show protective actions that look like jealousy. A cat might get upset if its owner pets another cat or even a dog. The cat might meow loudly, jump in the lap, or swat at the rival. Cats are known to be territorial. They might see the home or even the owner as part of their territory. If they sense a newcomer, they might feel threatened and attempt to drive that newcomer away.

However, cats can be more subtle. They might not bark or whine, but instead they might hide or sulk. Some might knock objects off tables or scratch furniture as if to show annoyance. People who love cats often say that their cat becomes standoffish if they return home after being around another cat, as if the cat senses another scent and does not approve.

Primates: Monkeys and Apes

Primates—such as monkeys, chimpanzees, and other apes—live in complex social groups. They have hierarchies and strong bonds. Because these animals can remember past events and form alliances, we see behaviors that strongly hint at jealousy and envy. For instance, a higher-ranked chimp might become upset if a lower-ranked chimp receives extra grooming or food. They might try to chase that chimp away or get attention from the one giving the grooming.

In some experiments, researchers taught monkeys to trade tokens for treats. If one monkey got a more tasty reward than another for the same token, the one who received the lesser reward often became agitated. They might refuse to keep trading tokens or throw the lesser reward back at the researcher. This reaction looks like envy or a sense of unfairness, which links closely to jealousy in group settings.

Among apes, jealousy might appear when two chimps have a close bond and a third tries to join. The original partner might show aggression or try to interfere. This behavior suggests that primates wish to protect their closeness, not wanting to lose it to a rival. It is not precisely the same as human jealousy, but it hints at a shared root in wanting to hold onto valuable social connections.

Birds and Bonding

Birds may not come to mind first, but some species form strong pair bonds. Parrots, for example, can become very attached to their human owners or to each other. Stories abound of parrots who become upset if they see their favorite person handling another bird. They might squawk, try to get between them, or peck at the rival. In wild settings, certain birds keep the same mate season after season. When a rival approaches, the bonded pair might chase the intruder away, squawking or flapping in what looks like anger or alarm.

Some bird owners say that if they talk to or pet another bird, the first bird acts restless or tries to reclaim attention by talking loudly or climbing onto the owner. While we cannot ask the bird, "Are you jealous?" their behavior suggests they do not like sharing the bond. In nature, losing a mate can mean losing help with gathering food or caring for offspring, so protecting that bond is important.

Horses, Cows, and Farm Animals

Farm animals, such as horses or cows, also show signs of protective behavior. Horses, for instance, are social herd animals. If they form a bond with a specific person who rides or grooms them, they might become stressed or rowdy when that person focuses on another horse. Some horse owners notice that their horse pins its ears back or pushes the second horse away. This could be seen as the horse trying to keep the bond exclusive.

Cows can show slight forms of rivalry in a herd, competing for the best feeding spot or the caretaker's attention if the caretaker often brings treats. While we might not call it jealousy in the human sense, it still suggests a wish to keep resources and affection for themselves. These behaviors can be mild, like nuzzling up to the caretaker, or more forceful, like pushing other cows aside.

Dolphins and Whales

Marine mammals, such as dolphins, are known for their high intelligence and social structures. Dolphins live in pods where they form close ties. Researchers have noted that dolphins sometimes show signs of rivalry if a member of the pod interacts too much with a newcomer. They might herd or chase away the intruder. They may also try to maintain physical contact with the one they are bonded to, which can look like they are saying, "Stay near me, not them."

Whales, though harder to study closely, also appear to have strong social connections. Some species, like orcas, live in family groups for much of their lives. While direct observations of jealousy in whales are rarer, their strong bonds suggest they could show protective behavior if they feel an important relationship is threatened. More research is needed to confirm the depth of these feelings, but the patterns hint that complex social mammals share many emotional traits with us.

Why Would Animals Evolve Jealousy?

Jealousy, at its core, is about protecting something valuable from being taken away. For social animals, this could be a mate who helps raise offspring, a caretaker who provides food or grooming, or a friend who offers support in fights or while hunting. In evolutionary terms, if an animal loses a key bond, it might lower its chances of survival or passing on genes. Jealousy, then, acts as a warning: "Protect what is yours before it slips away."

In pack or herd life, animals that react quickly to a threat might keep their resources or ally. Over many generations, those with a tendency toward protective behavior could pass on those traits. This does not mean animals have a deep, human-like thought process of "I must hold onto my mate or I will be sad." Rather, they have instincts or responses that help them guard bonds or items that matter for their well-being.

Comparing Animal and Human Jealousy

Human jealousy can involve complicated thoughts about the past, present, and future. We might worry endlessly about what might happen next, or remember times we were hurt before. Animal jealousy usually appears in the moment. A dog sees its owner pet another dog and reacts right away. It might not spend hours fretting afterward, although it can hold onto some memory of being upset if a certain pattern repeats.

Despite these differences, seeing jealousy-like behaviors in animals reminds us that this emotion has deep roots in social life. The building blocks—protecting close ties and resources—exist in many species. Our complex brains add layers of language, long-term planning, and reflection, making jealousy more intense or far-reaching in humans. But the core sense of "Hey, that is mine" or "Do not leave me out" can be recognized in many creatures.

Research Methods

To confirm that animals display jealousy-like responses, scientists design careful studies. For example, they might place an animal in a scenario where its caretaker pays special attention to another animal or even an inanimate object. They film the animal's actions to see if it tries to interrupt or shows signs of stress. If the behavior is much stronger than in a control condition—where the caretaker does not show that attention—researchers can link it to jealousy.

In group-living animals, scientists observe normal social behavior, noting how the animals react to others forming alliances. If an ape becomes aggressive when its close friend grooms another ape for too long, that might be recorded as jealous or competitive behavior. Researchers also watch for signs like changes in posture, vocal calls, or attempts to pull the friend away.

It is tricky, though, because we cannot ask animals how they feel. Scientists rely on behavior patterns and comparisons with known human displays of jealousy. Not all experts agree on what to call these animal behaviors. Some prefer terms like "resource guarding" or "social stress." Others say it is fair to use the word "jealousy," as the actions match what we see in people.

Managing Jealousy in Pets

Pet owners who notice jealous behaviors can take steps to reduce conflict. For instance, if a dog tries to push another dog away from the owner, the owner can give both dogs attention at the same time. This might teach the jealous dog that it is not losing anything by letting the other dog get petted. Another trick is to reward calm behavior. If the jealous dog sits quietly and waits, it gets a treat or praise.

When introducing a new pet, owners can be sure to give their old pet some special time or treats, so the old pet does not feel replaced. Creating separate feeding areas or resting spots can also lower the stress. In short, making sure each pet has enough attention and resources can reduce the chance of jealous outbursts.

Wild Animals and Their Hierarchies

In the wild, many species arrange themselves in hierarchies. The top individuals get first pick of food or mates, while lower-ranked ones have to wait. This can spark envy-like behavior, as a middle-ranked animal might challenge a higher-ranked one. Sometimes these challenges lead to fights. At other times, the lower-ranked animal might try to form alliances to climb up the social ladder.

While this might look like raw competition rather than jealousy, the line can be blurry. If a once-dominant animal sees another rising in status, it may try to reclaim or guard its position. The result can be attention-getting displays, such as chest beating in gorillas or vocal calls in certain monkeys. The aim seems to be to remind others, "I am still important here," which parallels jealousy in humans who fear being replaced.

Cases of Unfairness and Envy

We might also see signs of envy among animals. Envy is a feeling that arises when someone else has something we want. It can overlap with jealousy when that something is a resource or attention. Researchers testing monkeys with different treats found that if one monkey sees another monkey getting better treats for the same task, it may refuse to keep participating. The monkey might throw the lesser treat back, as if saying, "This is not fair!"

Parrots have also been studied in tasks that measure fairness. If a parrot observes another parrot receiving a reward for a certain action while it gets nothing for doing the same action, the first parrot might stop cooperating. Some see this as a sign of fairness concerns, which is linked to envy and jealousy. While we cannot be certain they have the same thoughts we do about fairness, these actions show animals notice differences and can react strongly to them.

Emotion or Instinct?

One question that often comes up is whether animals truly feel jealousy as an emotion, or if it is just an instinctual set of behaviors. Scientists have found that many animals have brain structures similar to those that shape human emotions. For example, the amygdala, which is involved in fear and other strong feelings, exists in many mammal species. The presence of these structures suggests animals might experience emotional states, though they might not label them the way humans do.

Animals also produce hormones like oxytocin, related to bonding, and cortisol, related to stress, which can affect how they behave in social scenarios. When an animal is in a situation that threatens its bond or status, these hormones might rise, leading to protective or aggressive actions. Whether we call it a true emotion or an instinct might be a matter of definitions, but the result is often similar to what we label jealousy in humans.

Lessons for Understanding Ourselves

Seeing jealousy-like behaviors in animals can tell us a lot about our own emotions. First, it reminds us that jealousy might have deep biological roots tied to survival in social groups. Protecting our relationships or resources can help us or our offspring thrive. Second, it shows that while we may think of jealousy as purely negative, it probably serves a purpose—telling us when we feel threatened, so we can respond.

At the same time, humans have advanced thought processes that animals lack. We can spin stories in our heads, imagine worst-case scenarios, and hold onto fears long after the moment has passed. This can make our jealousy more complex and sometimes more harmful. Animals might snap at a rival in the present moment, but then move on. Humans can stew over jealousy for weeks, months, or years, which can hurt our well-being and relationships.

By watching how animals react, we might also learn simpler ways to calm jealous feelings—like ensuring each family member or friend feels included, or giving attention evenly if we have more than one close bond. In the wild, balance and clear signals often keep the peace. In our own lives, honest talk and equal treatment can achieve something similar.

The Moral Side of Animal Emotions

Some people argue that if animals can feel jealousy or envy, we should think more carefully about how we treat them. A dog that feels jealous might also feel sadness or stress when left out. A monkey that senses unfair treatment might suffer emotionally. Understanding that animals can experience these states encourages many to advocate for better care of pets, farm animals, and wildlife. They say that ignoring the emotional life of animals overlooks an important part of their well-being.

Others caution that we should not place human labels on animals too easily. They point out that animals live by instincts that do not always match human values. An animal that is "jealous" might simply be fighting for resources, showing no moral awareness of fairness. Either way, studying jealousy in animals pushes us to be more mindful of how we interact with them and how we structure their environments.

Future Directions

The study of animal emotions is growing. With new methods, such as brain scans on certain animals or more detailed observations in natural habitats, we can get a clearer picture of how strong these feelings are. For instance, scientists might measure hormone changes when an animal's favorite companion interacts with another. They can also look at the long-term bonds in species like elephants or wolves to see how protective behavior shapes group life.

As we gain insight, we might discover that jealousy exists in more species than we once assumed. We might also find that some species show no signs of it, hinting at different social structures or survival strategies. Either outcome will deepen our understanding of how emotions guide animal behavior and how those behaviors overlap with our own emotional world.

Conclusion

Jealousy, long seen as a purely human trait, appears to have parallels in many parts of the animal kingdom. Dogs, cats, primates, birds, and even some farm animals show behaviors that resemble protecting a valued bond or resource from a real or imagined rival. Though animals do not reflect on these feelings the way humans do, the core action—guarding what matters—seems consistent.

By studying jealousy in animals, we see that this emotion may have developed as a way to keep valuable connections or items. It serves a need in social life, whether that is a dog seeking an owner's care, a monkey guarding a friend's grooming time, or a bird protecting its mate. Our own jealousy likely springs from the same root, even if it has grown more elaborate through our larger brains and complex societies.

Yet, there is a difference in scale. Humans can worry about a partner's devotion or a friend's success for months or years, fueled by memories and assumptions. Animals act more in the present. Recognizing this can help us handle our jealousy better. We might learn from animals to pay attention to the real, immediate threat (if any) and address it simply, rather than letting our minds spin painful stories.

Chapter 11: Recognizing Jealousy

Jealousy often begins quietly, with small thoughts or uneasy feelings that can creep into your mind. Maybe you notice a tightness in your stomach or chest when you see someone getting attention you wanted. Perhaps you find yourself daydreaming about how you might lose something special. If you are not sure what is happening, it can be easy to mistake these signals for sadness or anger. This chapter focuses on ways to recognize jealousy both in yourself and in the people around you. By noticing the signs early, you can avoid letting these feelings grow until they cause real damage.

Early Clues in Your Own Body

Our bodies often sense jealousy before we fully realize it. This might come as a quick rush of heat to your face or a flutter in your stomach. You might clench your fists without meaning to or start breathing more rapidly. These changes happen because, deep down, you are feeling threatened. Your body responds by getting ready to "fight or flee," just as if you were facing a physical danger.

Paying attention to these signals can help you name jealousy before it grows too big. You can practice by doing quick "body checks." If you suddenly feel tense or uneasy when you see a friend laughing with someone else, pause and note your reaction:

- Is your heart beating faster?
- Are your shoulders stiff or raised?
- Do you feel warmer than usual?

If the answer is yes, it might be a sign that jealousy is peeking out. Recognizing this in the moment lets you take steps to calm yourself. Perhaps you can step away and do some slow breathing or remind yourself that a single conversation between your friend and someone else does not automatically mean they will forget about you.

Spotting Unhelpful Thoughts

Along with physical signals, jealousy can show up as recurring thoughts or worries. For instance, you might catch yourself thinking:

- "She will like them more than she likes me."
- "I will get pushed aside."
- "They are so much better at everything than I am."

These thoughts might replay in your mind, even when you want to focus on something else. You might find yourself feeling a bit angry or sad toward the person you see as a rival, even if they did nothing to harm you. This kind of thinking can become a cycle: the more you worry, the more uneasy you feel, which then feeds more worry.

A helpful tool is learning to question these thoughts. When you notice a jealous idea popping up, try asking, "Is there real proof of this?" or "Am I imagining the worst?" Often, you might realize that you have no solid evidence and are simply afraid of a possibility. Just that small step can make the jealous thought less powerful. It does not mean the emotion goes away instantly, but it might not grow as large.

Changes in Behavior

Behavioral changes are another sign of jealousy. Maybe you start hovering around a friend or partner, checking in on them more than you usually do. You might ask a lot of questions like, "Where were you?" or "Who were you talking to?" without a real need to know. Or you might do the opposite, acting distant or cold. In either case, you are reacting to the uneasy feeling of being threatened.

You could also become more watchful on social media, noticing who likes or comments on your friend's posts. This is a clue that jealousy is pushing you to gather "clues," even if there is nothing actually suspicious going on. If you find yourself double-checking someone's online activity, ask whether you are doing this because you have a real concern or because you are feeling insecure.

In families, a child might pout, throw a tantrum, or refuse to share. In adult settings, a person might become sarcastic or critical. These behaviors can come from that hidden fear that something important is slipping away. By noting these actions in yourself, you can catch jealousy early and choose a better way to respond.

Emotional Clues in Others

Recognizing jealousy in someone else can help prevent misunderstandings. People might not say, "I am jealous," but their actions or tone may show it. For instance, a friend who normally jokes with you might become quieter or snap at you when you mention a new friend. A coworker who used to share tips might suddenly withhold information if they see you succeeding. A sibling might roll their eyes whenever a parent praises you, or leave the room when you talk about your achievements.

If you suspect jealousy, you might approach the person kindly. You could say something like, "I sense you are upset. Do you want to talk about it?" or "Is everything okay? You seem quieter than usual." This gentle invitation can open the door for them to share how they feel. While not everyone will admit jealousy, showing that you care can lessen the tension. Sometimes, a little compassion is enough for them to realize they do not have to compete with you.

Physical Signs in Others

Just as your own body might show jealousy, other people's bodies give hints too. You might see a tight jaw, folded arms, or a forced smile. They might shift their posture away from the person they perceive as a rival or fiddle with their hands, looking uneasy. If you notice these signs in someone who usually seems relaxed, it could suggest they are fighting some unpleasant feelings—possibly jealousy.

Of course, many emotions can cause discomfort. They might be stressed about an unrelated problem or simply having a bad day. It is important not to jump to conclusions right away. But if you see these clues around situations where attention or praise is at play, jealousy may be part of what they are feeling.

Mixed Feelings

Jealousy can come along with a mix of other emotions. For example, you might feel sadness if you believe you are losing something. You might feel anger if you think someone is stepping into your space. You might even feel shame for having jealous thoughts in the first place. This can create confusion: "Am I sad, mad, or jealous?"

Sorting out these mixed feelings can be tough, but it helps to ask: "What do I think I might lose?" If the answer is someone's care, respect, or a sense of belonging, jealousy might be at the root. Recognizing that does not make the other feelings vanish, but it points you to the main cause—fear of loss. Once you see that is the source, you can better address it, perhaps by talking to the person or finding ways to boost your self-esteem.

Self-Reflection

Jealousy can make you see things differently. You might notice yourself thinking poorly about a friend or loved one, imagining they are doing things on purpose. A helpful exercise is to step back and remember other times your mind might have blown something out of proportion. How often were your worst fears actually true?

Sometimes, keeping a small journal of your feelings can help. Write down moments when jealousy arises, including what you thought and how your body felt. Later, read what you wrote and see if those fears came to pass. This can help you see patterns. Maybe you realize you always feel jealous when you have had a stressful day, or maybe you see that your jealous worries rarely match reality. Recognizing these patterns is a step toward handling jealousy more calmly.

Triggers in Your Environment

Different situations can spark jealous thoughts. For some people, it might be social media posts of friends hanging out without them. For others, it could be seeing a sibling praised at a family gathering. Some might feel a twist in their gut if they hear their partner mention a funny coworker. By learning your triggers, you can predict when jealousy might pop up.

Knowing these triggers is not about avoiding them completely—life happens. But it can help you prepare. If you know a party is coming where your friend will be with new people, you can remind yourself beforehand that this does not mean you will be forgotten. If you know your sibling often gets praised at holiday meals, you can practice staying calm and reminding yourself that your worth does not depend on outdoing them. This sort of mental preparation can lessen the shock when the moment arrives.

Recognizing Subtle Jealousy

Sometimes, jealousy hides under other names. You might think you are just annoyed by your friend's new hobby, but deep down, you feel left out. Or you might say you are bored when you see your sibling's good news on social media, but actually you feel uneasy about not achieving something similar. These subtle forms of jealousy can be harder to spot because you might not even realize you are feeling threatened.

A good way to detect subtle jealousy is to ask, "Why does this bother me?" If there is no logical reason, or if the reason ties to being afraid the person is moving on without you, it might be jealousy in disguise. Admitting this to yourself can be uncomfortable, but it allows you to address it directly rather than hiding it under phrases like, "I just do not like what they are doing."

Group Settings and Peer Influence

When you are in a group—like a set of friends or coworkers—jealousy can build if you feel others are getting more attention or praise than you. Sometimes, one person in the group might get singled out as the "best," and that can sting. You might find yourself criticizing that person behind their back or feeling happy if they mess up. These behaviors hint that jealousy is present.

Pay attention to your own reactions in group situations. Do you get an urge to compete or prove yourself whenever someone else is praised? Do you feel relief when you see someone else not doing well? These are clues you might be dealing with jealousy. Spotting that can help you replace those negative urges with more positive actions, like learning from the person's strengths instead of wanting them to fail.

Overlapping with Envy

Jealousy and envy can feel similar but are not quite the same. Envy often means you want something someone else has—like a shiny new phone or a natural talent. Jealousy, in contrast, often involves a fear of losing what you already have. Still, they can mix. You might envy a friend's success while also worrying that they will not have time for you anymore. The key is looking at whether you feel threatened that something is slipping away.

Being aware of the difference can help you figure out what is happening inside. If you are mostly focused on wanting what someone has, that is envy. If you are mostly worried they will replace or ignore you, that is jealousy. Recognizing which feeling is present can guide you toward how to respond. For envy, you might work on appreciating what you do have, or on your own goals. For jealousy, you might focus on talking openly about your fears and strengthening trust.

Questions to Ask Yourself

When trying to spot jealousy in your life, here are some questions that can guide you:

1. **What exactly do I fear losing?**
   If you can name it—whether it is a friendship, a place in a group, or someone's attention—you might see that fear more clearly.
2. **Do I have proof that my fear is real, or am I guessing?**
   Often, jealousy grows from guesses. Checking the facts can keep it from getting bigger without reason.
3. **Have I felt this way before in a similar situation?**
   Recognizing patterns in your life can show how jealousy may be repeating, giving you clues on how to address it.

4. **Is there a better way to respond?**
   Before jealousy pushes you to do something you might regret—like sending a rude message—ask if there is a calmer path.

Times When Jealousy Is Positive

While jealousy can be harmful, there are moments when noticing it is helpful. For instance, if you feel jealous because your friend is spending less time with you, that might prompt you to realize you want to be closer to them. This can lead to a healthy conversation where you say, "I miss you. Can we plan something together?" Recognizing that you care about the friendship might help you take positive action.

In some cases, mild jealousy can push you to improve yourself. Suppose you see a friend getting applause for a skill you wish you had. You feel a pang of envy or jealousy because you fear they are "leaving you behind." Noticing this might spark you to practice or learn a new skill so you can share in their success. The key is to keep that drive healthy, not turning it into bitterness toward the friend.

The Downside of Ignoring Jealousy

If you pretend jealousy is not there, it can quietly grow. It might show up in passive-aggressive comments, cold shoulders, or hidden anger that breaks out unexpectedly. People sometimes push jealousy aside because it feels wrong to admit they are insecure. Yet ignoring it does not fix it. It can make problems between friends or family members worse in the long run.

A better approach is to be honest—at least with yourself—about feeling jealous. Acknowledging it allows you to decide what to do next. You might realize that talking to someone or making a small change in your own life is all it takes to calm your fears. If you bottle it up, you miss that chance for a solution.

Talking to a Trusted Person

Sometimes, simply sharing how you feel with a trusted friend or family member helps you see jealousy in a new light. You might explain the situation, and the other person can offer an outside view. They might say, "It sounds like you really value your friend, and you are just scared of losing them," or "Actually, I have seen them treat you with a lot of kindness. Maybe they are not leaving you out."

Hearing this perspective can ground you. It can also keep you from doing something rash out of jealousy. Just be sure the person you talk to is someone you trust to listen without judgment. If they make fun of your feelings, that can lead you to hide jealousy even more.

When Jealousy Needs Professional Help

In most cases, jealousy is a normal emotion that passes once we talk things through or make changes. However, if jealousy is causing serious trouble in your relationships or making you feel constantly upset, it might help to speak with a counselor or therapist. A professional can help you look at underlying reasons for your fears. Perhaps past experiences are fueling your current worries, or maybe you struggle with self-esteem that causes you to believe others will always leave you behind. Working through these issues can lighten the weight of jealousy.

It does not have to be a long or complex process. Even a few sessions can give you tools to recognize and handle jealous thoughts. This might include learning relaxation methods, practicing assertive communication, or building your sense of self-worth.

Putting It All Together

Recognizing jealousy is about noticing what your body, mind, and actions are telling you. It means being honest with yourself when you feel threatened, rather than hiding behind anger or denial. It also involves looking at the behavior of those around you. Sometimes, a person's sudden coldness or irritation might actually be a sign of jealousy. A bit of compassion from you could help them open up or calm down.

By staying alert to these signs, you can stop jealousy from growing into a bigger problem. Early steps might include taking a deep breath, questioning your assumptions, and talking things out calmly. If you do this, jealousy does not have to take over your life. Instead, it can serve as a reminder that you value certain connections or achievements, prompting you to care for them in a healthy way.

Recognizing jealousy is the first step toward handling it wisely. Once you see it, you can choose what to do next—whether that means clearing up misunderstandings, sharing your feelings, or adjusting your own view. Although jealousy can be unpleasant, catching it early can make a big difference, keeping your ties with friends, family, and loved ones intact and more trusting.

Chapter 12: Jealousy at School

School is a place where young people spend many hours each week, learning academic subjects but also building friendships and discovering who they are. It is no surprise, then, that jealous feelings often appear there. Students might compare grades, looks, popularity, or sports abilities. They might fear losing a best friend or not getting the teacher's approval. This chapter explores common reasons for jealousy at school, signs to watch for, and ways to handle these feelings so they do not overwhelm the learning environment.

Why School Breeds Jealousy

In many schools, there can be a strong focus on performance—getting top grades or excelling at sports. Students might be aware of who the "smartest" or "fastest" kids are, leading others to compare themselves. Teachers sometimes hand out awards or praise, and while that can motivate students, it can also spark jealous thoughts among classmates who feel left behind.

Social groups also matter a lot. Friendships can shift as people meet new classmates or discover new interests. If your best friend starts sitting with a different group, it is normal to feel a pinch of jealousy. A fear arises: "Are they replacing me? Am I not important anymore?" Social media adds another layer. Classmates might post pictures of a get-together you were not invited to, leaving you feeling left out. All these pressures can combine and make jealousy quite common in the school setting.

Common Triggers in the Classroom

1. **Grades and Test Scores**
   Some students become jealous if they see classmates scoring higher than them. They might wonder, "How did they do so well without seeming to study?" Others might be jealous of classmates who get praised by the teacher for good work. These jealous thoughts can build tension in study groups or lead to resentful feelings toward higher-scoring peers.

2. **Popularity and Friend Circles**
   Many schools have social groups seen as "popular," while others might feel invisible. A student who used to be in the spotlight might become jealous if a new student arrives and captures everyone's attention. Or someone who wants to fit in might feel jealous watching others gather in a circle without them.
3. **Teacher's Approval**
   Teachers can unintentionally cause jealousy if they openly favor certain students. Maybe a teacher often calls on the same student or praises their answers in class. Others might feel overlooked, wondering why they do not get the same spotlight. This can lead to envy or anger directed at the teacher's favorite.
4. **Team Sports**
   When students try out for sports teams, some get chosen, others do not. Even among those who make the team, some might get more play time. A student stuck on the bench might feel jealous of the star player. They might question why the coach gives that player special chances.
5. **Talents and Skills**
   Schools often host talent shows or encourage students to share their abilities in music, art, or debate. Seeing someone else sing beautifully or draw an amazing picture might spark jealousy. A student could feel overshadowed if their own talents do not get the same notice.

Physical and Emotional Signs

Just like other forms of jealousy, school-related jealousy can show up in how you feel and how you act. Some students might become critical, saying things like, "They only got those grades by cheating," or "She is only popular because she buys fancy clothes." These negative comments can be a clue that the speaker is jealous. Others might withdraw and become quiet, feeling as though they cannot compete, so why try?

Physically, a student might get tense or upset when report cards are passed out or when a certain teacher gives praise. They might clench their jaw or tap their foot anxiously. If you notice these signs in yourself, it could mean school jealousy is brewing. For instance, if you find your heart pounding whenever the teacher asks someone else to demonstrate a skill, it might be that you wish you were in their shoes.

Friendships and Jealousy

Friends are a big part of school life. Sometimes, you and a friend might do everything together, only for one friend to meet new people and drift away. This can leave the other feeling abandoned or second best. If this is you, you might start acting cold toward your friend or speaking badly about the new group they are hanging out with. This behavior, while understandable, can push your friend further away.

A healthier approach is to talk openly. Let your friend know that you miss them. Ask if you can still plan some time together. It might turn out that their new friendships do not replace you at all—they simply want to expand their circle. By being honest, you give them a chance to reassure you. If, however, they truly have moved on, you can try to accept that relationships change. It might be sad, but it also frees you to form new bonds without grudges or bitterness.

Navigating Group Projects

Group assignments can be stressful, especially if some classmates are seen as "smarter" or more hard-working. If you feel jealous because a particular student is praised as the "leader" in your group, it can cause silent conflicts. You might start ignoring their ideas or refusing to cooperate. If the teacher notices the tension, it can harm your grade or cause even more friction.

Instead, try to split tasks in a fair way. If a certain student is strong in one area—like organizing data—maybe they handle that part. You can shine in another area, such as making visuals or presenting. When each person's strengths are recognized, there is less reason for jealousy. Communicate clearly, sharing thoughts like, "I would love to handle the speech part; I feel confident there." This approach respects your abilities and theirs, lowering the risk of feeling overshadowed.

Bullying Rooted in Jealousy

Sometimes, jealousy at school can turn into bullying. A student might tease or mock someone who is getting good grades or who is well-liked by teachers and peers. They might spread rumors to bring that person down. This form of bullying can stem from a wish to level the playing field by hurting the target's reputation. If you see this happening to you or someone else, it is important to speak up.

Let a teacher or counselor know if jealousy-fueled bullying is taking place. Bullies might be acting out because they do not believe they can succeed in a kinder way. By addressing it early, you can keep the atmosphere safer. Teachers, principals, or other staff might step in to help the bully understand that this is not the solution, and they might encourage them to find healthier ways to feel good about themselves.

Handling Comparison

Comparison at school can be tricky. It is easy to notice who gets top grades, who runs the fastest, or who seems to have the biggest friend circle. One way to handle these comparisons is to remember that everyone has strengths and weaknesses. The person who aces math might struggle with writing. The person who is the best on the basketball team might not do as well in music class. Keeping this balanced view can lower the urge to be jealous.

You can also try focusing on your personal improvement. If you want better grades, aim to beat your own past scores, not necessarily the highest scorer in class. If you want to get better at sports, measure how much you improve from one month to the next. By focusing on your own growth, you reduce the stress of trying to surpass someone else just for the sake of it.

Talking to Teachers and Counselors

If you feel overwhelmed by jealousy—maybe it is causing fights with classmates or affecting your mood—do not hesitate to talk to a teacher or school counselor. They are trained to help with social and emotional issues, not just academic problems. You can say something like, "I keep feeling upset when my friend does better than me in class, and it is messing up our friendship. Do you have any advice?"

Teachers might suggest studying together with the friend you envy, turning the rivalry into a shared effort to learn. Counselors can guide you with exercises to boost your self-confidence, so you do not view another's success as a threat to you. They can also help if you are on the receiving end of someone else's jealous behavior, offering ways to cope with envy-based teasing or hostility.

Building Healthy Friend Groups

The best friend groups at school are ones where each member is valued. No one has to stand above the others in every skill or area. In such groups, if someone does well, the others feel happy for them rather than threatened. Building this kind of support might take time, but you can start by offering genuine praise when a friend succeeds. For instance, if your friend gets picked for the school play, congratulate them instead of secretly feeling resentful.

When you do well, accept your friends' praise but also show interest in their goals. Ask, "How is your soccer practice going?" or "How did your big test turn out?" This back-and-forth care can keep jealousy at bay. If everyone feels recognized, there is less reason to be jealous. Over time, you might see that you can celebrate one another without worrying about losing status.

Online Schooling and Jealousy

Some students attend online classes or blended programs. Surprisingly, jealousy can still pop up there. You might see classmates posting projects or grades in group chats. You might notice your teacher praising someone's typed response in a live session. Or you might watch your best online friend playing games with others and fear you are being left out.

The same rules apply: watch for signals in yourself that you are jealous, and try talking about it if you feel it is harming your relationships. Online groups can be just as tight-knit, and it is still possible to create an environment where success is shared rather than fought over. Setting up study or gaming sessions where everyone can join can lower the fear that a friend group is forming without you.

Balancing Activities

In a busy school life, you might juggle homework, clubs, sports, and time with friends. Sometimes jealousy comes from not having enough time to do what you want. You might see another classmate who seems to manage it all and wonder, "How do they have time for everything?" Instead of feeling jealous, you can look at whether you can plan your days differently. Perhaps you can cut back on one activity to focus on what truly matters to you.

If you feel jealous because a classmate is shining in too many areas, remember that people have different paces. They might be juggling more than you realize, or they might have help at home that you do not have. Trying to copy their schedule might not work for you. Concentrate on using your time wisely in a way that meets your own goals and needs. This mindset can help you worry less about matching others.

Supporting Others Who Feel Jealous

You might notice a friend growing distant or making negative remarks about you because they are jealous. In that case, try to be kind. You could say, "It feels like something is off between us. Did I do something to upset you?" If they open up and admit jealousy, you can assure them that you still value them. Maybe you can invite them to join an activity you are doing well in, or you can praise something they do better than you. This does not mean you must shrink yourself to make them feel better, but a bit of empathy can help them see they are not being pushed out.

Handling School Events

Events like dances, talent shows, or academic contests can heighten jealousy. You might be jealous of someone who is going to the dance with a certain person or someone who wins a school speech competition. Prepare yourself by focusing on what you can control. If you like someone and want to go to the dance together, speak up early instead of stewing over it. If you want to do well in a contest, put in the effort rather than just hoping you will outperform others.

Even if things do not go your way—say, someone else wins or the person you like goes to the dance with somebody else—it can help to handle your disappointment without aiming negative comments at them. School events are supposed to be enjoyed. By choosing maturity, you avoid letting jealousy become a wedge between you and classmates.

When Jealousy Interferes with Learning

In extreme cases, jealousy can stop you from focusing in class. You might daydream about how to "beat" a rival or feel so upset you cannot concentrate on the teacher's lesson. If that happens, recognize it as a problem. Your education should come before any rivalry. Talk to a counselor, parent, or teacher about strategies to refocus. Some students find it helps to have goals written down: "Today, I will learn Chapter 3 in math, and I will not compare my grade to anyone else's." Sticking to clear aims can keep your mind on learning instead of jealousy.

Self-Care and Positive Habits

Taking care of yourself physically and emotionally can lower jealous thoughts. If you are always tired or hungry, you might be more prone to negative feelings. So try to get enough sleep, eat balanced meals, and take short breaks to clear your head. Activities like gentle exercise, listening to music you enjoy, or keeping a simple hobby can help you feel more settled in yourself.

Another way to manage your feelings is to keep a short list of the things you are proud of. This is not bragging; it is reminding yourself that you do have achievements and good qualities. When you see a classmate do something impressive and feel that twinge of jealousy, glance at your list. It might calm you to remember that you have your own strengths too.

Accepting Differences

Schools bring together people of many backgrounds and talents. Not everyone has the same resources or support at home. Some might have a tutor, while others do not. Some might have family members who coach them in sports or pay for special lessons. This can make a big difference in how well they do. Recognizing these differences can help you see that success is not always a simple race. People start from different spots.

At the same time, if you do have advantages, try not to flaunt them in a way that makes others feel small. Being modest about your achievements can help maintain good relationships. Celebrate them privately or with close friends and family, and be respectful about how you share them at school. This does not mean you cannot be happy for your achievements—just be mindful of how others might feel if they are already struggling.

The Bigger Picture

Most students will finish school and move on to the wider world, whether that is more education or a job. The things you feel jealous about in school might not matter much after you graduate. The big test that someone aced while you scored lower could be less important once you have your diploma. The popular crowd might drift in different directions, and your place in that social ranking might fade away.

Keeping this bigger picture in mind can help shrink jealousy. It does not mean that your current feelings are not real, but it can offer comfort. You have a long future ahead, full of chances to shine in your own way. School is just one chapter of your life.

Conclusion

Jealousy at school is normal. It happens when students compare grades, social status, or talents. It might involve worrying about losing a friend to another group or feeling overshadowed by classmates who stand out. Recognizing these feelings in yourself or in others can help you choose better responses—like talking openly, setting personal goals, or seeking help from teachers and counselors.

Chapter 13: Jealousy at Work

Workplaces bring together people with different skills, goals, and personalities. In these settings, jealousy can flare when someone believes a coworker has an advantage, is getting special praise, or is on a faster track to success. While jobs are meant for earning a living and contributing our best efforts, human feelings do not vanish at the office door. In this chapter, we will look at what fuels jealousy at work, how it can harm teams, and steps people can take to handle these situations before they cause bigger problems.

Why Jealousy Appears at Work

A job is more than just a place to earn money. It is also a setting where people build identities, form friendships, and measure their own progress. If someone feels another person is racing ahead or getting more kindness from the boss, jealous feelings might arise. A few key factors play into this:

1. **Competition for Promotions:**
   In many workplaces, there are limited spots at higher levels. If one person is chosen for a raise or a new role, others may feel left behind. This can spark thoughts like, "Why not me?" or "What do they have that I don't?"
2. **Different Treatment by Leaders:**
   Sometimes, managers or bosses seem to favor certain employees. They might praise them openly or give them choice tasks. Others who do not get that same warmth might feel jealous, fearing they will never get the same chance.
3. **Recognition and Credit:**
   Work can involve group projects, but if one person's efforts are singled out, others might feel overlooked. If the spotlight falls on the same person again and again, jealousy can grow among the rest of the team.
4. **Pay and Perks:**
   Pay differences or extra benefits, like better schedules or nicer equipment, might create suspicion. Employees might wonder if a coworker's better pay or privileges come from some hidden favoritism rather than clear, fair rules.

5. **Personal Insecurity:**
   Some people are more prone to jealousy because they are not sure of their own abilities. They might think a coworker's success will highlight their own flaws. This can make them overly watchful of others' achievements.

Signs of Jealousy Among Coworkers

Jealous feelings at work do not always show up as open conflict. Often, they come out in subtle ways. Here are some signs that jealousy might be present:

1. **Avoiding Teamwork:**
   A jealous coworker might skip team efforts or refuse to share information, trying to keep others from shining.
2. **Backhanded Compliments or Comments:**
   A person might say something that sounds nice on the surface, but has a slight sting to it. For example, "Wow, you are doing so well for someone who just got here," could be hiding jealousy behind a smile.
3. **Spreading Rumors or Gossip:**
   Sometimes, jealousy drives people to whisper negative stories about a coworker. They may try to paint that person in a bad light to the rest of the office.
4. **Withholding Help:**
   A jealous individual might ignore requests for assistance or "forget" to pass on important messages, hoping the other person will fail.
5. **Feeling Secretly Glad About Others' Mistakes:**
   If a coworker looks happy when someone else's project faces a setback, that can hint at jealousy. They might think it levels the field or gives them a better chance.
6. **Silent Competition:**
   Even without direct conflict, a jealous employee might rush to do tasks faster or stay late just to outdo the person they envy.

How Jealousy Hurts the Workplace

When jealousy grows unchecked, it can harm the entire work environment. Here are some ways it can cause trouble:

- **Lower Team Spirit:**
  If people do not trust each other because of jealous acts, morale can drop. This may lead to more stress, reduced sharing of ideas, and fewer friendly interactions.
- **Higher Turnover:**
  In toxic environments, good employees might quit rather than deal with constant tension. The company then loses talented people, and remaining workers feel the extra strain.
- **Poor Communication:**
  Jealous employees might hold back helpful tips or fail to tell teammates about important deadlines. This can delay projects and cause mistakes.
- **Stress and Anxiety:**
  Targets of jealousy may feel tense, worried they are being sabotaged or judged. The jealous person is also stressed, since they are always comparing themselves to someone else.
- **Blocked Growth:**
  A team where jealousy runs high may avoid new challenges or tasks because people are focused on protecting their own positions, not on learning or improving together.

Handling Personal Feelings of Jealousy

If you find yourself feeling jealous at work, it can be helpful to step back and identify the cause. Ask yourself:

1. **What Do I Want?**
   Is it a promotion, recognition, or simply to be accepted by your boss or coworkers?
2. **Is There Evidence of Unfair Treatment?**
   Or could it be that you are worrying about losing out based on assumptions?

3. **What Can I Do to Improve My Skills?**
   Rather than focusing on someone else's successes, consider ways to boost your own performance. Can you seek training, ask for feedback, or find a mentor?
4. **Can I Talk Calmly to Those Involved?**
   If you truly think someone else is getting special treatment unfairly, consider talking to a manager or HR department—but do it factually, without accusations driven by emotion.
5. **How Do I View My Worth?**
   Sometimes, jealousy can come from low self-esteem. Working on a healthier sense of self can help you feel less threatened by a coworker's achievements.

Approaching a Jealous Coworker

If you sense a coworker is jealous of you, you can attempt a friendly approach:

- **Offer Collaboration:**
  Suggest working together on a small project. This can help them see that your achievements are not meant to push them down.
- **Give Genuine Compliments:**
  If there is something your coworker does well, let them know. A kind word might help them feel recognized.
- **Stay Patient and Polite:**
  Even if their actions feel hurtful, responding with anger can fuel a cycle of negativity. Set firm boundaries if needed, but do not attack them.
- **Document Issues:**
  If a jealous coworker's actions cross the line into harassment or sabotage, keep a record. This can include saved emails or notes on incidents. If the problem grows, you might need to share evidence with a manager or HR.
- **Do Not Show Off:**
  If you know a coworker is sensitive about your successes, it might be wise to avoid boasting. You do not have to hide your good work, but you can be mindful of how you share it.

The Role of Leaders and Managers

Managers and bosses have a big influence on whether jealousy thrives or fades. They can reduce jealous feelings by:

1. **Being Fair and Transparent:**
   If employees understand how raises, bonuses, or promotions are decided, there is less room for guesswork. Fair systems also make it harder for people to suspect secret favoritism.
2. **Sharing Praise Evenly:**
   Leaders should notice and commend different team members for their efforts, not just the same high achiever all the time. This helps everyone feel appreciated.
3. **Setting Team Goals:**
   When a group shares a target—such as completing a project by a certain date—members are more likely to bond and help each other, reducing rivalry.
4. **Encouraging Skill Development:**
   Offering training or mentorship can give people paths to improve. This way, they do not see one person as always ahead with no way to catch up.
5. **Listening to Concerns:**
   Employees should feel safe bringing up jealousy-related problems. Managers who listen with an open mind can address issues before they escalate.
6. **Promoting a Positive Culture:**
   Team-building activities, clear communication, and an inclusive attitude can go a long way in preventing jealousy from taking root.

Creating a Cooperative Environment

To lessen jealousy at work, it helps if the whole team fosters cooperation. This can be done through:

- **Group Projects with Shared Credit:**
  Make sure everyone's part is recognized. If one person does most of the work, be sure to reward them appropriately, but also highlight what each member contributed.

- **Buddy or Mentor Systems:**
  Pair up newer employees with more experienced ones. This turns potential envy into a learning exchange.
- **Regular Check-Ins:**
  Team meetings where people can raise issues or share progress prevent hidden resentments from building up.

When coworkers see each other more as allies than rivals, jealousy has less room to grow.

Handling Jealousy in Different Work Settings

Jealousy can appear in many types of jobs—offices, factories, restaurants, or remote teams. Here are some particular considerations:

1. **Office Jobs:**
   These often involve promotions and performance reviews. If the path for growth is unclear, or if only a few roles are available, competition might become fierce. Clear guidelines from managers help a lot.
2. **Creative Fields:**
   Writers, artists, or designers might compare their ideas, styles, or recognition. A supportive environment that values different styles can reduce jealousy.
3. **Shift-Based Work:**
   In places like retail or healthcare, workers might compete for the best shifts or days off. Managers who rotate schedules fairly can lower jealous complaints.
4. **Remote Teams:**
   People working from home might see only the final outcomes of projects, and it can be easy to imagine others are doing better. Video calls or group chats where each member shares updates can promote transparency.
5. **Small Businesses:**
   In a tiny team, each person's role is often visible. If the boss gives special attention to a friend or family member, jealousy might flare quickly. Setting clear job descriptions and progress steps can prevent suspicion.

The Personal Toll of Jealousy

Jealousy at work not only damages relationships with others; it also affects the jealous person's well-being. Constant comparison can lead to:

- **Stress and Worry:**
  Always checking what a coworker is doing can be tiring, robbing you of focus on your tasks.
- **Lower Confidence:**
  If you are stuck thinking about someone else's achievements, you might forget your own strengths.
- **Missed Growth:**
  Jealousy can blind you to real opportunities for learning. If you are busy comparing, you might miss a chance to join a workshop, sign up for a new project, or ask for helpful advice.

Healthy Ways to Deal with Feelings

If you find jealousy creeping into your work thoughts, you can try these actions:

1. **Name It:**
   Admitting that you feel jealous is the first step to handling it. It is normal to feel insecure sometimes; acknowledging it helps you move forward.
2. **Write It Down:**
   A simple way is to jot down what is triggering your jealousy. Is it a coworker's praise from a manager? Is it a new task they got that you did not? Seeing it on paper can make it less overwhelming.
3. **Flip Your View:**
   If a coworker succeeded, think about how it might help the team or even you personally. Could their new position bring more business or lighten your load in some way?
4. **Reach Out:**
   Talk to a friend outside work or a mentor. Share what is happening. They might offer a view that calms you or point out ways to improve your situation.
5. **Set Personal Goals:**
   Focus on what you can control—your own progress. Break down your

tasks into steps and celebrate small wins (in a quiet, personal sense, not using our banned terms or synonyms). This can shift your mind from envy to self-betterment.

6. **Practice Gratitude:**
   Think about what you do have—a steady job, supportive peers, or interesting tasks. That might lessen the sting of watching someone else get a nod from the boss.

Knowing When to Seek Help

Some jealousy problems can be too big to tackle alone. If you notice any of the following, it may be time to speak with a boss, an HR representative, or even a counselor:

- **The environment feels hostile or unsafe:**
  If jealous coworkers are spreading false rumors, stealing credit for your work, or harassing you, you should not face this by yourself.
- **You cannot get your work done:**
  If jealousy drains your energy so much that your tasks suffer or you dread going to work, professional help or a serious talk with management might be needed.
- **It is causing personal distress:**
  Feeling anxious, losing sleep, or always on edge because of workplace jealousy suggests you need support. A counselor can help you sort through these feelings and build coping skills.

Success Stories: Turning Jealousy Around

While jealousy can seem like a dead end, there are stories of teams turning it into something positive. For example, imagine a sales team where one member always closed the biggest deals. The others felt jealous and frustrated. Instead of letting this grow into open rivalry, the manager asked the top seller to share strategies with the rest. The top seller gave tips, explained how they followed up with leads, and even went with coworkers to a few meetings. Over time, each member improved. The jealousy became less important because they saw that the star teammate was an ally, not a threat.

In another case, a junior employee was jealous of a senior employee's frequent praise. Rather than seething in silence, the junior worker asked if the senior could mentor them. By watching how the senior prepared, wrote reports, and spoke with clients, the junior worker got better. Meanwhile, the senior found pride in helping someone. Their bond turned from potential friction into a supportive relationship.

Company Culture as a Shield Against Jealousy

Organizations that build a culture of respect and fair treatment have an easier time fighting jealousy. Some ways to strengthen this culture include:

- **Clear Advancement Paths:**
  Outline what is needed for promotions or raises. This way, employees see a path forward based on performance, not favoritism.
- **Frequent Feedback:**
  Instead of waiting for annual reviews, managers can give short, regular insights on each person's work. This helps employees know where they stand and how to improve.
- **Team Celebrations of Milestones:**
  If the team reaches a sales target, for example, the recognition should note everyone's role. This shows that success is shared and not just about one person.
- **Conflict Resolution Training:**
  Teaching employees how to talk about disagreements can prevent jealous feelings from turning into full-blown fights.
- **Leader Role Model:**
  If leaders show they value each person's efforts, employees learn to do the same. Leaders who practice fairness, openness, and kindness set the tone.

Moving Forward

Jealousy at work can be draining, but it does not have to run the show. By recognizing the signs, taking steps to manage personal feelings, and working toward a supportive environment, coworkers can reduce the tensions that envy brings. Teams work better when members see each other's achievements as part of a bigger success story rather than a reason to feel threatened.

Your job should be a place where you can learn, grow, and build a satisfying career, not a battleground of comparisons. If you face jealousy—whether your own or from someone else—take heart that many have navigated this challenge and come out with healthier work ties. With open talk, fairness, and a focus on real growth, workplaces can become supportive communities rather than zones of silent rivalry.

Chapter 14: Effects of Jealousy on Emotions

Jealousy might seem like a single emotion, but it often stirs up a swirl of other feelings. It can make you feel anxious about the future or sad about losing something you value. It might spark anger if you think someone is stepping into your space or ignoring your needs. In this chapter, we will examine how jealousy affects different emotions, how it can show up in the body, and the possible long-term costs if it goes unchecked. By the end, you will see that jealousy is not just one feeling, but a bundle of signals that can shape how you see yourself and others.

A Tangle of Emotions

Jealousy is often explained as the fear of losing something to someone else, but it can overlap with many other emotional states:

1. **Anxiety:**
   Jealousy can make you worry about what might happen. You might play scenarios in your mind—imagining a friend never speaking to you again, or a partner leaving you. This constant worry can lead to racing thoughts and trouble sleeping.
2. **Sadness:**
   If you truly believe you will lose someone's care or attention, it can bring sorrow. You might grieve something that has not even been lost yet, feeling like you are already missing out.
3. **Anger or Resentment:**
   Jealousy sometimes brings up anger toward the person who seems to be causing the threat. You might feel annoyed at a coworker who gets a promotion, a friend who spends time with someone else, or a sibling who gets praised.
4. **Guilt or Shame:**
   When people realize they are feeling jealous, they might be ashamed. They could think, "Why am I acting so insecure? I should be happy for them." This shame can cause them to hide the jealousy or pretend everything is fine.

5. **Insecurity:**
   Deep down, jealousy can stem from feeling not good enough. Seeing someone else do well might highlight your own doubts.
6. **Relief (When Resolved):**
   On a positive note, once you talk through jealous fears and see they are untrue or fixable, you may feel a huge sense of relief.

Physical Effects on the Body

Like many strong emotions, jealousy can trigger physical changes. Some of these are similar to what you feel when afraid:

- **Increased Heart Rate:**
  You might feel your heart pounding if you think you are losing something precious.
- **Tense Muscles:**
  The body readies itself to fight or defend, leaving you feeling stiff or restless.
- **Upset Stomach or Nausea:**
  Strong emotional stress can upset your digestive system.
- **Perspiration or Clammy Hands:**
  Stress hormones can make you sweat more.
- **Quick Breathing:**
  In moments of panic or worry, you might breathe shallowly.

If these symptoms happen often because of ongoing jealousy, they can wear you down, leading to stress-related issues like headaches or trouble sleeping.

Effects on Self-Esteem

Jealousy can greatly affect how you see yourself. If you fear someone is better than you or that you might be replaced, it can lower your sense of worth. You might feel:

- **Doubt About Your Abilities:**
  "They are better at everything; I must have no talent."

- **Comparisons:**
  "Look how happy they are. Why can't I be like that?"
- **Fear of Trying New Things:**
  If you worry about being judged or overshadowed, you might not take chances to learn or improve.

Over time, these thoughts can become a loop. The more jealous you feel, the more you doubt yourself, and the easier it is for jealousy to flare up next time. Breaking this loop often involves seeing your own strengths and remembering that someone else's success does not erase yours.

Influence on Relationships

Jealousy can strain all sorts of relationships:

- **Friendships:**
  If you constantly doubt your friend's loyalty, you may act clingy or push them away with accusations. They might feel tired of explaining themselves.
- **Family Ties:**
  A sibling who always hears snide remarks about their successes might distance themselves. Parents might not know why their children fight.
- **Romantic Bonds:**
  Partners can feel smothered if one is always suspicious. Trust might crumble if jealousy is never addressed.
- **Coworkers or Teammates:**
  Jealousy can turn a healthy workplace into a tense one, as people compete or quietly resent each other.

On the other hand, a little jealousy can be a reminder that you care. It may prompt you to show appreciation or talk openly. The key is how you manage it. If both sides communicate and respect each other's feelings, they can often overcome small bouts of jealousy and even learn something about how much their bond matters.

Emotional Exhaustion

When jealousy is ongoing, it drains a person's emotional energy. They might find themselves:

- **Mentally Tired:**
  Constantly thinking about "what ifs" leaves little room for creative or positive thoughts.
- **Socially Withdrawn:**
  Feeling jealous can make people avoid events or gatherings where they might see someone else in the spotlight.
- **Disconnected:**
  If they believe they are always second place, they might stop trying to connect with friends or loved ones.

Prolonged emotional exhaustion can lead to mood swings, where a person snaps at small things or feels sad for no clear reason. It can also pave the way for deeper mental health struggles like anxiety disorders or depression if not addressed.

Ripple Effects on Daily Life

Jealousy does not limit itself to moments around the feared loss. It can spill into other parts of your life:

1. **Reduced Focus on Tasks:**
   Thinking about your friend's new bond or your coworker's promotion might distract you from your own responsibilities. You could end up making mistakes or taking longer to finish tasks.
2. **Trouble Enjoying Good Moments:**
   Even if something nice happens to you, jealousy can lurk in the background. You might worry that someone else's success is bigger, spoiling your own contentment.
3. **Impact on Physical Health:**
   Stress hormones released by jealousy can, over time, add to health risks. This might mean more frequent colds, higher blood pressure, or tension headaches.

4. **Missed Chances for Growth:**
   If you are busy comparing yourself to others, you might avoid learning from them or teaming up with them. You lose possible mentors, friends, or allies.

The Role of Thoughts

One reason jealousy can stick around is that we feed it with repeated thoughts. Maybe you replay a scene in your mind: "They gave that person more applause than me." Or "She laughed at his joke so much—maybe she likes him better." Each replay of the thought can tighten jealousy's grip. It is as if you are practicing being jealous, teaching your mind to keep that feeling going.

Recognizing this mental habit is the first step. You can challenge it by asking:

- "Is there any real proof that something is happening?"
- "Could this have a simple explanation?"
- "Am I mixing past hurts into a new situation?"

Learning to let go of repeated thoughts is not always easy, but even small steps help. Some people use mindfulness exercises, focusing on the present moment rather than diving into worries. Others talk their concerns through with a friend who can offer a more balanced view.

Short Bursts vs. Long-Term Jealousy

Jealousy can come in quick bursts or develop into a long-term pattern:

- **Short Bursts:**
  You see your friend with someone else, feel a pang of jealousy, then realize it is probably no big deal. This moment passes, and you move on.
- **Long-Term Patterns:**
  You might always be suspicious or worried that you are not good enough. Each time a small event happens—like someone else getting praise—your jealousy flares. Over weeks, months, or years, this can create deep ruts in your emotional well-being.

Short bursts can be handled by a quick check, a calming reminder, or a simple talk with the person involved. Long-term patterns often need more thoughtful steps, such as seeking professional help, journaling, or working on self-esteem. Recognizing which pattern you are in can guide your next move.

When Jealousy Becomes Harmful

While jealousy is a normal emotion, it can become harmful if it pushes someone to act in destructive ways:

1. **Controlling Behavior:**
   Demanding to see a partner's phone, telling a friend whom they can or cannot talk to, or placing limits on a loved one's freedom are signs that jealousy has crossed a boundary.
2. **Lashing Out:**
   Yelling at someone or physically hurting them because of a jealous thought is not acceptable.
3. **Spreading Lies:**
   If a jealous person starts rumors to damage the person they envy, it can create serious harm and break trust.
4. **Self-Harm or Withdrawal:**
   Some people blame themselves deeply, thinking they are worthless if they feel replaced. This can lead them to harm themselves or isolate completely.

If jealousy leads to these actions, it is crucial to seek help immediately—whether from trusted friends, family members, or professionals.

Finding a Healthier Balance

Jealousy can be a sign that you value something—a relationship, a goal, or a status in someone's life. Recognizing this value can be your starting point. For instance, if you see a friend spending time with new people and you feel jealous, this might mean you really care about that bond. Instead of letting the feeling eat away at you, try:

- **Open Communication:**
  Say, "I miss hanging out with you. Can we plan something?"
- **Request Reassurance (In Moderation):**
  A little check-in can be healthy, such as asking, "We are still on good terms, right?" But repeated questioning can become draining for the other person, so find a middle ground.
- **Plan Quality Moments:**
  Instead of focusing on who else they see, create your own special times together. This could be simple, like chatting over lunch or playing a game you both enjoy.
- **Work on Self-Worth:**
  Remind yourself that you are not just the sum of this one bond. You have other skills, interests, and people who value you.

Turning Jealousy into Motivation

Sometimes, jealousy signals a desire for something. If you envy a friend's athletic skill, maybe you really do want to learn that sport. Or if you are jealous of a coworker's easy way with the boss, maybe you want to build stronger communication skills. Rather than letting the negative side of jealousy linger, you can channel that energy:

1. **Set a Goal:**
   What specific skill or outcome do you want to achieve?
2. **Make a Plan:**
   Could you take a class, practice with a friend, or read about the skill?
3. **Take Small Steps:**
   Aim for realistic goals—like improving a bit each week—rather than expecting to catch up all at once.
4. **Track Progress:**
   Notice your own improvement. This can remind you that growth is possible, even if you are not at the same level as the person you envied.

In this way, jealousy becomes a signal that helps you see what you care about. By acting on that care constructively, you reduce the sense of helplessness and build confidence.

Coping Strategies When Feelings Flare

If you feel jealousy rising suddenly, you can use these quick coping strategies:

- **Deep Breaths:**
  Inhale slowly for a count of four, hold for a moment, then exhale for a count of four. Repeat a few times.
- **Distraction:**
  Focus on an activity you enjoy—listen to music, read a favorite book, or do something creative.
- **Positive Self-Talk:**
  Tell yourself, "I can handle this. I am worthy."
- **Physical Movement:**
  A short walk or a few stretches can calm the rush of stress hormones.
- **Stay Off Social Media (Briefly):**
  If seeing certain posts fuels jealousy, take a break until you feel calmer.

The Long-Term Cost of Unresolved Jealousy

If jealousy remains unresolved over months or years, it can deeply affect a person's life:

- **Strained or Lost Relationships:**
  Friends, partners, or family members might walk away if constant jealousy makes interactions stressful.
- **Missed Learning Chances:**
  Envy can stop you from asking a skilled person for help or trying new experiences.
- **Constant Self-Doubt:**
  You might start to feel everything you do is overshadowed by others.
- **Increased Risk of Mental Health Problems:**
  Continuous stress can contribute to anxiety or depression, especially if you feel trapped in these thoughts.

The good news is that people can and do break free from long-term jealousy. Often, it starts by acknowledging that the emotion is real and that it stems from certain fears or insecurities. From there, strategies like counseling, open talks, self-improvement, and stress reduction can make a noticeable difference.

Building Emotional Awareness

To handle jealousy's many layers, improving emotional awareness is helpful. This includes:

- **Naming Feelings:**
  Instead of saying, "I feel bad," try to identify the feeling: "I feel afraid I will be forgotten" or "I feel angry because I think they are ignoring me."
- **Understanding Triggers:**
  Does your jealousy spike when you see someone get praised? When your partner texts someone else? When your sibling shares good news? Recognizing triggers can help you be prepared.
- **Checking Your Thoughts:**
  Ask, "Could I be interpreting this wrong?" or "What if there is another explanation?"
- **Staying Present:**
  If you start spinning out with "what if" fears, gently guide your mind to what is happening right now. Are you actually losing something, or is it an imagined possibility?

Reaching Out for Support

You do not have to face jealousy alone. If you have a trusted friend, parent, teacher, or counselor, sharing your worries can lighten the load. They might say, "I have felt that too," or offer a viewpoint that makes the fear less strong. If the jealousy centers on a relationship, inviting the other person to talk might open the door to reassurance. Hearing them say, "I am not leaving you out," can be enough to quiet your mind.

In more serious cases, mental health professionals can help you explore the root of your jealousy. Maybe it is tied to an old experience where you felt abandoned or compared. Therapists can guide you in breaking unhelpful thinking loops, teaching you skills to respond better when you feel jealous.

Looking Ahead

Jealousy can change your emotional world, stirring up anxiety, anger, or sadness. It can disturb your sleep, shift your focus from daily tasks, and damage your ties with people you care about. Yet it is also a normal human emotion that signals you value something. By seeing jealousy for what it is—a mix of feelings pointing to a fear of loss—you can learn to handle it with understanding and care.

When you accept that jealousy can pop up at times, you stop treating it as a terrible flaw. You can then focus on managing it in healthy ways: talking openly, staying mindful of your thinking patterns, and taking small steps toward self-improvement. Over time, you might even see jealousy as a teacher—a sign that something matters to you. With self-reflection and kindness, both to yourself and to others, the strong waves of jealousy can calm, leaving you more at peace with your feelings and relationships.

By dealing with jealousy thoughtfully, you protect your emotional health. You also keep your bonds strong, letting your friends, family, or coworkers know that you respect them without letting fear drive a wedge between you. Jealousy does not have to define your life. With the right tools and support, you can recognize and channel it in a way that fosters honest connections and a steady sense of self-worth.

Chapter 15: Ways to Handle Jealousy

Jealousy can be tricky and unpleasant, but it does not have to stay that way. People can learn ways to manage it, keep it small, or even turn it into a sign of something they truly value. While it takes practice, the good news is that anyone can get better at handling these feelings. In this chapter, we will look at practical steps you can take when you notice jealous thoughts, so you do not become stuck in fear or anger. We will also talk about how to handle jealousy in different parts of life—within friendships, at work, or among family members—without repeating what we have already explored in the book.

---

1. Identify What You Feel and Why

When you sense a rush of worry, anger, or sadness in connection with someone else, pause and ask: "Is this jealousy?" Recognizing it is the first step. You might think:

- "I am afraid my friend likes someone else more than me."
- "I am upset because my coworker gets more credit than I do."
- "I feel uneasy about how much time my partner spends talking to someone else."

Naming it out loud or in your mind helps you pinpoint jealousy instead of brushing it aside or mixing it with other emotions. Once you know it is jealousy, think about the deeper reason for it. Are you worried about being left out? Do you feel insecure about your own skills? Pinpointing the root cause can shine a light on what you really want—maybe more reassurance, more recognition, or a sense of worth.

Digging Deeper

Sometimes, the main cause of jealousy is not what you see on the surface. A sibling's new award might stir up old feelings of being overshadowed. A friend's change in behavior might tap into a fear of abandonment from past experiences. By taking a moment to think about the background of your jealousy, you may discover that it is tied to something personal. This is not about blaming yourself; it is about understanding your emotional history so you can respond in a clear way.

2. Practice Self-Soothing Techniques

Once you catch that jealous feeling, you can use small actions to soothe yourself. Simple practices can interrupt the spiral of anxious thoughts and calm your nerves.

- **Breathing Exercise:**
  Close your eyes, take a slow breath in through your nose, and exhale gently. Count to four as you breathe in, hold for a second or two, then breathe out for four counts. Repeat a few times.
- **Grounding Technique:**
  Look around and notice a few things: a color you see, a sound you hear, or a texture you feel under your feet. This shifts your focus from fearful thinking to the present moment.
- **Positive Self-Talk:**
  Say calming words to yourself, such as, "I am safe," or "I can handle this feeling." It might sound simple, but it can remind you that jealousy is just an emotion, not the entire story.

These exercises help you step out of the flood of thoughts. Even if your heart is racing, your mind can learn to slow down and view the situation with a bit more calm.

---

3. Challenge Negative Assumptions

Jealous thoughts can twist your view. You might jump to conclusions like, "They do not want me around anymore," or "My coworker is trying to push me out." Before you fully believe these ideas, ask for proof. Questions to consider:

- "What actual signs do I have to support this worry?"
- "Is there any other way to see the situation?"
- "Am I mixing past hurts with what is happening now?"

You might find that you are filling in gaps with guesses. For instance, your friend might be talking to someone else more often because they are working on a joint project, not because they prefer that person over you. By stopping to look for actual clues, you reduce the power of jealous assumptions.

4. Seek Clarification, Not Conflict

If your jealousy involves another person, you can try talking to them calmly. The key is to share your feelings in a clear way, without accusing them. Instead of saying, "Why are you ignoring me?" you could say, "I have been feeling uneasy. Did something change between us?" This opens a door for honest conversation rather than an argument.

1. **Explain Your Feelings:**
   For example, "I feel worried that we are not spending as much time together. I value our bond, and I am scared I might lose it."
2. **Ask for Their View:**
   "Have you noticed any shift? Is there something going on that I do not know about?"
3. **Stay Open:**
   Listen calmly, even if they say things you find surprising. They might have no idea you felt left out, or they might be going through personal changes.

Bringing up your concerns early can stop jealousy from growing too large. Sometimes, just hearing the other person's side can settle your mind.

---

5. Explore What You Can Do Differently

When jealousy strikes, you can focus on changes in your own actions rather than trying to control someone else. For instance:

- **Build Your Skills or Knowledge:**
  If you feel jealous of a coworker's successes, could you learn new methods or ask for guidance that might help you do your job better?
- **Strengthen Communication:**
  If you are worried about a friend drifting away, make an effort to reach out and plan an activity.
- **Set Boundaries:**
  If a relative's praise for one sibling feels unfair, think about ways you can calmly share your feelings with your parent or sibling. You could say, "I appreciate that you notice my sibling's strengths. Could you also let me know what I do well?"

Focusing on your own growth or communication keeps you from feeling helpless. It turns the energy of jealousy into a push for self-improvement or problem-solving.

6. Share Your Concern with a Supportive Person

Sometimes, just telling a friend or trusted person how you feel can take away some of the sting. Pick someone who will listen without judgment—maybe a mentor, a family member, or a teacher. Lay out your worries, like, "I feel jealous because my classmate seems to get special attention from the teacher. I am worried it means I am falling behind." Hearing their perspective can help you see things more clearly.

If your jealousy is tied to a personal relationship, you could also talk with a professional counselor if it feels too big to handle alone. Counselors have experience helping people manage complex emotions. They can guide you to figure out if your fears are based on real threats or old insecurities.

7. Use "I" Statements

In any tense discussion related to jealousy, try to avoid pointing fingers with "you" statements like, "You always do this," or "You never think of me." Instead, use "I" statements:

- "I feel worried when you do not reply to my messages for days."
- "I feel small when the teacher praises you and not me."
- "I am uneasy about how close you seem with that coworker."

This style of expression focuses on your feelings rather than blaming them. It also invites the other person to understand you better. People are more likely to respond kindly when they do not feel attacked.

8. Keep a Journal of Progress

Writing your thoughts in a notebook can help you see changes over time. Each day or week, jot down when you felt jealous and what helped you handle it. Also record when jealousy was not a problem—maybe you saw a friend doing well and felt happy for them, or you watched a sibling get recognized and felt okay. Noticing these small victories can give you a sense of improvement and remind you that jealousy does not control you.

Over time, you might find that certain patterns pop up. For example, you might see that you usually get jealous when you are tired or stressed. Or maybe it happens more during times when you have not seen your friends for a while. Recognizing these patterns helps you prepare and handle jealousy before it grows.

---

9. Try to See Someone Else's Success as Inspiration

When you see someone excelling, your first response might be, "I wish that were me," or "I cannot match that." Instead, consider another angle: maybe their success can show you what is possible. If you feel jealous of a coworker's achievement, see if they can share any tips. If you envy a classmate's talents, ask for insights about how they practice. Turning jealousy into curiosity can shift your feelings from envy to interest.

Even if you do not fully walk the same path as them, you can learn something from observing how they stay motivated or solve problems. This does not mean copying someone else. It means noticing what works and then shaping your own approach. By changing jealousy into admiration, you build a friend or ally rather than a rival.

---

10. Respect the Other Person's Freedom

Jealousy can sometimes lead to attempts to control what others do. You might feel tempted to say, "Do not hang out with them," or "Do not talk to that coworker." This rarely works out well. People often dislike feeling restricted, and it can cause resentment. Instead, remember that each person has the right to form their own friendships or do their tasks at work. If you think there is a real issue, talk gently, but trying to bar them from their choices can break trust.

This does not mean you have to let someone hurt you or treat you badly. If a situation truly crosses a line, you have a right to speak up or set clear boundaries for yourself. The key is distinguishing between genuine problems and normal interactions that simply make you uneasy.

---

11. Practice Self-Worth

Much jealousy stems from feeling "not good enough." Building a stronger sense of self-worth can reduce that worry. Think about areas in your life where you shine, even if they are small. Maybe you are great at fixing broken items around the house or listening to a friend's troubles. If you can appreciate these skills, you might feel less threatened by someone else's achievements.

You can also affirm your good qualities with statements like, "I am a caring friend," "I am improving at my sport," or "I can handle new challenges at work." Such positive reminders do not mean ignoring your flaws. They simply balance out the negatives and show you that you have strengths worth noticing. The more you trust your value, the less jealous you tend to be.

---

12. Limit Your Comparisons

These days, it is easy to compare yourself to others—especially online. Social media might show only the best parts of someone else's life, leading you to think they have everything you lack. Cutting back on this type of comparison can help. If you find yourself scrolling through posts that spark envy, take a break or unfollow certain accounts.

In real-life settings, comparing yourself to a friend or coworker day in and day out can wear you down. If you see them as a "rival," everything they do becomes a threat. A different approach is to see each person as on their own path. Their path might have ups and downs you do not see. By freeing yourself from constant comparisons, you let your own progress unfold in a healthier way.

13. Learn from Past Moments of Jealousy

Everyone has felt jealous at one time or another. You might recall moments as a kid when you were jealous of a sibling's toy or a classmate's trophy. How did you handle it then, and what would you do differently now? Thinking back can show you what methods helped and which made the situation worse. Maybe you learned that throwing a tantrum only made people upset, while calmly talking got you somewhere.

Revisiting these memories can remind you that jealousy is normal but not permanent. You might realize that some things you once envied do not matter much now. That sense of time passing can give you perspective. What seems huge in the present might fade later.

14. Embrace Healthy Outlets

When jealousy brings frustration, you can channel that energy into something constructive:

- **Creative Projects:**
  Paint, draw, or write a story when you feel uneasy. Let those emotions flow onto the page or canvas.
- **Physical Activity:**
  Run, dance, do a sport, or follow a fitness routine. Physical movement can relieve tension built up by strong emotions.
- **Community Service:**
  Helping others can bring a sense of purpose. It also shifts your focus away from "What am I lacking?" to "How can I give?"

These outlets are not about ignoring jealousy; they are ways to handle the energy that jealousy stirs up, so it does not boil over and harm your relationships.

15. Small Wins

Notice when you manage jealousy in a healthy way, even if it is a tiny step. For example, if you felt jealous of a coworker's praise but kept your cool, took a breath, and congratulated them anyway, that is progress. If you saw your friend hanging out with new people and did not let that spiral into panic, it is worth recognizing. These small victories show you can respond calmly.

---

16. Avoid Oversharing Your Jealousy

While it is good to seek support from a trusted friend or counselor, telling everyone at length about your jealous worries can lead to uncomfortable outcomes. Spreading your concerns might cause misunderstandings or give others the wrong impression about you or the person you feel envious about. Choose your confidants wisely—someone who can keep things private and offer balanced views.

In a work setting, for instance, it is better to speak privately to a manager or HR if jealousy leads to conflicts. Broadcasting your feelings to all your colleagues might increase workplace tension. In a family, it might help to speak to a parent or a sibling you trust, not every relative. Keep the circle small, focusing on the people who can help you manage the emotion wisely.

---

17. Know When Professional Help Is Needed

Jealousy can become severe if it shows up too often or makes daily life hard. For instance, if you check a partner's phone every hour or feel consumed by anger at a coworker's success, consider seeking advice from a mental health professional. Therapists understand how to deal with strong feelings. They can help you see patterns or past events that feed your jealousy.

In counseling, you might learn techniques such as cognitive restructuring, where you replace unhelpful thoughts with more realistic ones. Or you might practice role-playing scenarios to find better ways of communicating. Over time, you can turn jealousy from a constant problem into just an occasional signal that something needs attention.

18. Forgive Yourself if You Slip

Even with the best methods, you may still have moments where you act on jealous feelings in a way you regret—maybe snapping at a friend, sending a snippy text, or ignoring someone you care about. When this happens, realize it does not wipe out all your progress. Everyone slips up sometimes. The key is to apologize if you hurt someone, reflect on the experience, and learn from it.

You might think, "I could have handled that better by asking questions instead of accusing them." This reflection can guide you to do better next time. Holding onto guilt will not help; turning the slip into a lesson will.

---

19. Encourage a Culture of Openness

In family settings, friendships, or work teams, you can promote an atmosphere where people feel safe sharing their concerns. If others see you calmly discussing moments of jealousy—like saying, "I have been feeling uneasy and need to talk about it"—they might feel inspired to do the same when they face similar feelings. This openness can lower tension all around.

For example, in a team at work, you could suggest regular check-ins where people talk about how they feel regarding workloads or recognition. In a family, you might gently encourage siblings to express when they think things are not fair, so parents can address it early. This approach helps prevent jealousy from growing in the dark.

---

20. Keep Perspective

Finally, remember that jealousy often focuses on a small slice of life. A friend might have a new achievement, but you do not see the challenges they face elsewhere. A coworker might get praise, but perhaps they are dealing with stress at home. When you sense jealousy creeping in, remind yourself that life is more than this one area where you feel behind or threatened.

Try to appreciate the bigger picture: your relationships, health, personal goals, and the many things you have learned and done so far. By keeping a broad view, you prevent jealousy from dominating your thoughts. You can be happy for what you do have while working toward what you want without fear.

Conclusion

Handling jealousy is a gradual process that can involve reflection, honest talk, and simple actions. There is no quick fix that makes jealousy disappear forever, since it is part of human emotions. However, you can change how you react to it. By learning to spot jealous feelings, soothing yourself, asking open questions, and building your self-worth, you reduce the power that jealousy has in your life.

You might find that jealousy even becomes a clue to important things you care about—like a reminder that you value a friendship, job role, or family bond. Instead of letting that worry eat you up, you can respond by strengthening what you already have and being open about your needs. Through patience and practice, jealousy can go from an overwhelming fear to a more manageable feeling that prompts honest discussions and positive changes.

Keep in mind that progress does not happen in a straight line. You might feel better one day, then get hit by a wave of jealous thoughts the next. That is normal. With the methods shared in this chapter—self-soothing, clear talk, staying open-minded, seeking support when needed—you can guide yourself back to calmer waters. Over time, these methods become second nature, helping you build stronger emotional balance and healthier connections with the people around you.

Chapter 16: Healthy Bonds Without Jealousy

Having safe, trusting connections in life can feel like a breath of fresh air. But many people wonder if it is truly possible to maintain bonds with little or no jealousy. While you may not be able to remove jealousy entirely—since it is a normal human emotion—you can shape your relationships in ways that keep jealous feelings minimal. In this chapter, we will look at how different kinds of bonds can be built on honesty, respect, and acceptance, making jealousy less likely to pop up or cause lasting damage. We will also explore how to spot and maintain a truly healthy connection, whether it is with friends, partners, coworkers, or family members.

---

1. Trust as the Foundation

Trust is the key to healthy bonds. It grows when people show consistent honesty and respect for each other's feelings. Over time, trust can become stronger than the occasional jolt of jealousy. For example, in a friendship, if you know your friend truly cares about you—even when they hang out with others—you might feel only a small pang of jealousy that quickly fades. You trust you are not being replaced.

In romantic relationships, trust comes from open conversations, being true to your word, and staying transparent about things like finances or big decisions. When partners trust each other, they usually do not jump to the conclusion that any new friend or coworker is a threat. Of course, trust does not appear overnight; it is something people build through daily choices, such as following through on promises, being kind, and listening carefully.

---

2. Respect for Individual Space

Even close bonds thrive when each person feels they have room to be themselves. This might mean time spent on personal hobbies, friendships that do not always include the partner, or a separate corner in the house for one's own tasks. When people can keep their identity and do not feel forced to give up personal interests, they are less likely to become jealous or make others jealous.

For instance, in a family, parents might allow children to explore their own interests, letting them join clubs or see friends without feeling threatened that the child loves someone else more. In adult relationships, encouraging each other to maintain friendships and private activities can show a level of respect that prevents jealousy. Giving space does not mean ignoring each other; it means trusting that love or friendship can handle short absences or separate interests.

3. Clear and Open Communication

Healthy bonds rely on open talk about wants, needs, and changes. When lines of communication are strong, jealous thoughts have less chance to grow in secret. If you feel uneasy about how often a friend sees someone else, you can bring it up calmly: "I am feeling left out. Could we plan some time together soon?" This direct approach is more effective than stewing silently or making passive-aggressive remarks.

In work teams, open communication helps people share credit and handle potential rivalries. For example, if you need extra help with a task, you should feel okay asking a coworker for advice without fearing they will mock you. Likewise, if you see tension building, you can talk openly at a meeting: "Let us share how we are feeling about recent changes so that we are on the same page." By shining light on concerns, you stop jealous feelings from growing in the shadows.

4. Support Rather Than Competition

In healthy bonds, people cheer each other on rather than feeling threatened by one another's growth. When you genuinely hope your friend or partner does well, jealousy fades because their success feels like a shared joy. This does not mean you never feel a tiny twinge of envy, but it is balanced by genuine happiness for them.

1. **Friends Supporting Each Other:**
   If your friend signs up for a competition and wins, you show excitement for them, knowing that their achievement does not reduce your worth.

2. **Families Cheering Each Other:**
   Siblings can learn to be glad when one excels, trusting that parents love them all in their own ways.
3. **Coworkers Teaming Up:**
   When a coworker receives praise, you can think, "This is good for our department," instead of feeling overshadowed.

Choosing to be glad for each other's wins makes a big difference. You remove the "one must lose for the other to gain" mindset, paving the way for a connection that feels safe and encouraging.

---

5. Recognizing Real vs. Imagined Threats

Healthy bonds often include the wisdom to know when a problem is real or just a guess. For example, you might notice your friend spending time with new people. Is that truly a signal that you are no longer important to them, or are you imagining the worst? In a strong relationship, you are comfortable asking gently, "You have been hanging out with them a lot. Are we still okay?"

Because trust is already there, your friend can answer, "Yes, I am just exploring a new hobby with them, but we are still good." You breathe easier, and jealousy does not balloon into an argument. If there was an actual concern—like they are upset with you—it can come out plainly, and you can solve it together. Solid relationships let you address these thoughts before they turn into bigger fears.

---

6. Valuing Each Person's Uniqueness

Jealousy often arises from comparison. In healthy bonds, people understand that each person has strengths and weaknesses. Rather than trying to outdo one another, they notice that differences add variety to the bond. One friend might be funny and outgoing, while the other is calm and thoughtful. One coworker might be quick at math, while another excels in creative tasks.

When you appreciate these differences, you reduce competition. You do not feel the need to prove you are "better" because you see how each person's skill fits into the bigger picture. This attitude helps close friends, family members, and teams function like puzzle pieces that fit together. Feeling valued for who you are makes jealousy less likely to take over.

7. Honoring Boundaries

Respecting someone's boundaries is an act of care. For instance, if a partner is not comfortable sharing personal details about an old relationship, pushing them might breed mistrust. Likewise, if a friend needs alone time every weekend to recharge, you respect that space instead of feeling hurt. Boundaries do not have to be walls; they are more like guidelines that keep relationships balanced.

In families, boundaries could be about how siblings handle personal items or how parents respect a teen's privacy. At work, it might mean respecting off-duty hours instead of bombarding coworkers with calls or messages. When people see their limits are respected, they feel secure, which helps keep jealousy at bay.

8. Handling Mistakes with Honesty and Forgiveness

No relationship is free of slip-ups. Someone might forget a promise or inadvertently spend too much time with a new friend. In healthy bonds, mistakes are faced head-on. The person at fault can say, "I am sorry I hurt your feelings," without excuses. The person who was hurt can respond with sincerity, like, "I appreciate you saying that, and I will work on letting this go."

By mending fences quickly, you stop small wounds from growing. This kind of honesty and forgiveness keeps jealousy from building. If you suspect your coworker took credit for your idea by mistake, you can talk with them calmly, and they can apologize or clarify, rather than letting bitterness grow in silence. This pattern of "recognize, repair, forgive" keeps the relationship strong.

9. Celebrating Strengths

When each person's efforts are noticed (in a simple way that avoids certain words we have been steering clear of), it breeds a feeling of fairness and shared respect. For a friend who starts a new project, you might acknowledge, "I see how hard you are working on that. Good job." For a sibling who does well at a sports event, you might say, "Your practice really shows." By focusing on actions and improvements rather than just results, you encourage a supportive bond.

The same is true in a team or workplace. When you see a coworker's contribution, acknowledge it, even if it is small. Let them know, "Your data check helped us avoid an error." These small acknowledgments make everyone feel seen and lower the possibility of hidden envy.

10. Balanced Give-and-Take

Strong bonds generally have a give-and-take flow. Friends help each other with problems, share responsibilities, and listen when the other is upset. Coworkers swap tasks if someone is swamped. Families make sure that chores and support do not always fall on the same person. When the load is shared, people feel more at ease, with less reason to envy a person's place in the group.

Of course, this does not mean everything is always split 50-50. Sometimes, one sibling might need more help, or one friend might need more emotional support. But over time, there is a balance. Each person can rely on the other without feeling like they are always giving or always taking. That sense of fairness helps minimize jealous thoughts like, "Why am I doing all the work while they relax?"

11. Encouraging Openness About Feelings

Even in healthy bonds, small jealous sparks can still appear. A family member might think another sibling is getting extra praise. A friend might be worried about a new friendship. A coworker could fear being overshadowed by a colleague's achievements. In a trusting environment, people can speak up about it gently: "I felt uneasy yesterday when you seemed to ignore me during the meeting."

By bringing it out in the open, you can clear the air and understand each other's viewpoints. This kind of emotional openness is easier when people already have a foundation of trust and kindness. It stops resentments from growing, so jealousy does not have a place to hide.

---

12. Willingness to Adapt

Life changes. People switch schools, move to new cities, change jobs, or start families. A bond that used to involve daily visits might shift to weekly phone calls. Healthy connections adapt rather than cling too tightly to the old ways. If a friend moves away for a job, you might switch to online calls and plan visits when possible. While change can spark jealousy ("They have a whole new life now"), a strong bond weathers these shifts with mutual support.

The same is true in families. When a sibling gets married or a parent remarries, the family structure changes. Adjusting to new routines takes patience and understanding, but open hearts can keep everyone close without harboring jealousy for the new people in the family circle.

---

13. Seeing Others' Lives as Their Own

One cause of jealousy is thinking we have a claim on someone else's time or success. But in healthy bonds, we realize that each person has their own path. Your sibling might do well in a field you do not find interesting, or your friend might spend more time on a new hobby that excites them. You can respect their path without feeling it takes away from yours.

Accepting that other people's choices reflect their own dreams lowers the chance of thinking, "They are doing this to push me aside." It reminds you that you do not have to measure your life against theirs. You are each free to do what suits you. If they reach a milestone, you can be glad they found what they love, and you can keep going on your own track.

---

14. Handling External Pressures

Sometimes, jealousy in a relationship does not come from inside the bond but from outside opinions. Maybe others compare siblings or talk about who is the "favorite." Perhaps friends outside the group stir drama by saying, "I heard they like Person A better than you." In a healthy bond, people recognize these outside pressures and do not let them wedge in.

You might respond to gossip calmly, "Thanks for letting me know, but I will talk to them directly if I am worried." Or you might reassure a sibling, "We both know Mom and Dad love us in different ways, not one more than the other." Staying firm in your own trust helps shield the relationship from negative outside voices that could spark jealousy.

---

15. Recognizing Abuse or Control

While this chapter focuses on healthy bonds, it is important to note that if someone tries to control you through jealousy—saying, "You cannot see your friends," or "You must show me your phone all the time"—that is not healthy. A good relationship does not demand that you cut off other connections or constantly prove your loyalty. If you feel trapped or controlled, that is a warning sign. You might need to speak to a trusted person or a counselor.

In a safe, balanced connection, each person respects the other's freedoms and encourages them to keep healthy ties with friends, family, or colleagues. People can discuss any concerns without demanding total control over each other's actions.

---

16. Simple Joy in Each Other's Company

In truly healthy connections, people genuinely like being around each other's presence. They share jokes, discuss daily ups and downs, and show kindness in normal conversations. Because they enjoy this time together, they do not worry every moment about what else the other person might be doing. Jealousy fades when you know that, whenever you do spend time together, it is good and helpful to both sides.

This does not mean they never have disagreements. But the overall feel is one of ease—like a comfortable home, where people trust that their place is secure. That sense of belonging can be enough to keep jealousy from arising often.

17. Long-Term Friendship Tips

For friendships that last years or even decades, jealousy might come and go. But if you want a bond to be steady and low in jealousy, keep a few ideas in mind:

1. **Stay in Touch:**
   Even simple messages or calls can show you still value each other, especially when life gets busy.
2. **Allow for Growth:**
   Friends will change. Accepting new stages in their life—like marriage, parenthood, new jobs—helps the friendship remain flexible.
3. **No Scorekeeping:**
   Avoid thinking, "I did something for them, now they owe me." Instead, trust that kindness goes both ways over time.

With these habits, your friendship can stand the test of time. Jealous feelings might pop up briefly, but they are overshadowed by the trust and goodwill you have built.

---

18. Family Harmony without Jealousy

Families often have their own struggles. Parents might worry about showing favor, siblings might compete for attention, and relatives might compare lifestyles. Yet healthy families can keep jealousy lower by:

- **Rotating Responsibilities:**
  Each sibling gets a turn to pick weekend activities, to feel important.
- **Shared Celebrations:**
  Family events that acknowledge each member's achievements, big or small, can keep one person from always hogging the spotlight.
- **Honest Talks:**
  If a child feels overshadowed, let them share that. Listen without dismissing their feelings.
- **Fair Opportunities:**
  If parents can, they offer similar chances (like lessons, trips, or resources) to each child according to their needs, to reduce the sense of unfairness.

A family that sees each member's uniqueness and works to keep fairness in decisions stands a better chance of avoiding long-lasting jealous feuds.

19. Workplace Bonds That Are Strong and Balanced

While work may not be where you form your closest personal connections, it is still a setting where healthy interactions matter. You can help keep jealousy low by:

1. **Offering to Help:**
   If you have expertise in an area, share it with your team. This reduces any idea that you are hoarding information.
2. **Accepting Help:**
   If a coworker offers guidance, say yes if you need it, and show gratitude. Collaboration can break down walls of envy.
3. **Spreading Praise:**
   If your project succeeded partly thanks to a teammate, mention them to the manager. Giving credit to others helps everyone feel included.
4. **Learning from Others' Wins:**
   When someone gets promoted, ask for tips on how they reached that point. That sets a tone of growth rather than resentment.

A group of colleagues who root for each other's progress makes the environment more enjoyable and reduces the tension that leads to jealousy.

---

20. Small Steps Toward Big Results

Creating healthy bonds without constant jealousy does not require a massive change overnight. It is often about consistent, small steps:

- **Listen Attentively:**
  Give eye contact, let others finish speaking, and show genuine interest.
- **Ask Before Assuming:**
  If you see something that bothers you, ask calmly rather than jumping to negative conclusions.
- **Offer Kindness:**
  A quick message or a friendly note of thanks can reassure people that they matter.
- **Practice Sharing:**
  Tell others what is going on in your life, too. Keeping relationships two-sided prevents jealousy from creeping in due to secrecy or distance.

Over time, these small acts build a pattern of trust and compassion, making jealousy less of a factor. You will still feel the occasional twinge, but it will have fewer places to grab hold if the relationship has become secure.

Conclusion

It is perfectly normal for a bit of jealousy to pop up in any relationship now and then. But when the bond is strong—rooted in trust, open talk, fairness, and respect—those feelings remain small and do not turn into major issues. By encouraging genuine care for each other's growth and dreams, people can make jealousy just a minor bump along the road rather than a daily barrier.

In healthy relationships, you see both sides freely offering understanding and kindness. People feel safe voicing concerns, knowing they will be heard rather than judged. They give each other space, trusting that closeness does not require holding on too tightly. They acknowledge each other's achievements, understanding that one person's success does not erase the other's worth.

These bonds are built on choices made day by day. Each time you listen rather than assume, each time you share your feelings rather than hide them, each time you give credit to others for their help, you strengthen the connection. Bit by bit, you create a relationship where jealousy has little room to grow. And if a spark of jealousy does appear, there is enough trust and goodwill to talk about it, fix misunderstandings, and move forward together.

In the end, aiming for healthy bonds without constant jealousy does not mean you never feel insecure. Instead, it means that when you do, you have the tools and understanding to handle it openly. You trust that the other person cares about you enough to hear your concerns. You believe in your own worth, so someone else's achievements or friendships do not leave you feeling empty. This creates bonds that are freer, kinder, and stronger—allowing everyone involved to thrive and enjoy the connection in a safe, steady way.

Chapter 17: Helping Others Face Jealousy

Jealousy is not always easy to spot if you are looking at it from the outside. People might hide their feelings behind forced smiles or small comments that carry a sharp edge. Yet, when someone you care about is struggling with jealousy, you can often sense that something is off. Maybe they avoid you, or maybe they become too clingy and critical. In this chapter, we will talk about how to help a friend, sibling, coworker, or other person handle their jealous thoughts without pushing them away. We will look at recognizing when someone is jealous, guiding them through tough feelings, and setting healthy limits for yourself in the process. By offering kindness and understanding, you can play a part in easing their jealousy and keeping your own sense of well-being.

---

1. Seeing the Signs of Jealousy in Someone Else

Before you can help, you have to notice that someone is jealous. They might not say so out loud, especially if they feel ashamed of being jealous. Still, a few signals might point you in that direction:

1. **Change in Tone or Behavior:**
   They were friendly before, but now they act distant, make sarcastic remarks, or ask suspicious questions.
2. **Comparisons or Put-Downs:**
   They say things like, "You got lucky," or "It must be nice to have everything so easy," when talking about your achievements.
3. **Pulling Away from Group Activities:**
   If you invite them out and they refuse with weak excuses, it might be that seeing you with others makes them uneasy.
4. **Overly Close Monitoring:**
   They might check your social media, ask who you are with, or keep track of your daily moves in a way that feels odd.
5. **Small Jabs or Undermining Comments:**
   They offer compliments that do not sound genuine, or they point out your flaws whenever you share good news.

If you pick up on these signs, do not jump to blame them right away. They might be dealing with low self-worth or fear of losing you. Some people even react in ways they barely understand. Recognizing that jealousy may be behind their words or actions is your first step toward helping.

2. Why It Matters to Offer Help

You might wonder why you should get involved if someone else is jealous. After all, is that not their personal problem? But if they are a friend, family member, or coworker, their jealousy can affect your bond or the entire group's mood. Helping them handle it can lead to:

- **Less Tension:**
  Clearing the air can stop silent resentments that grow into bigger rifts.
- **Better Teamwork or Harmony:**
  When jealousy eases, people can share ideas more openly. In families, it can end or reduce bickering.
- **A Stronger Connection:**
  If you guide them through a hard feeling, they may trust you more, knowing you are understanding rather than judgmental.
- **Personal Growth for Both of You:**
  Supporting someone encourages patience, empathy, and better conflict resolution skills on your side, too.

Of course, it is important not to take on responsibility for their feelings entirely. You can only do so much. But a caring approach can make a real difference if the person is willing to talk and work toward change.

3. Approaching the Issue Gently

When you sense jealousy is harming your bond, a calm talk might help. However, it can be touchy, because jealousy often brings up shame or insecurity in the person who feels it. Consider these tips when you start the conversation:

1. **Choose the Right Time:**
   A calm, private setting is better than trying to talk in a busy hallway or during a tense moment.

2. **Start with Empathy:**
   Open with something like, "I might be reading this wrong, but I sense you are upset. I care about you, and I want to understand what is bothering you."
3. **Use "I" Statements:**
   For example, "I have noticed you seem distant lately," rather than "You are acting so weird." This sounds less accusing.
4. **Listen More Than You Speak:**
   Once you have stated your observation, let them talk. They might open up slowly or test if you really want to hear them out.
5. **Acknowledge Their Feelings:**
   Saying, "It sounds like you have been feeling worried or hurt," can ease them into sharing more.

Your first goal is to open a door, not to fix everything right away. By showing patience, you let them feel safer in talking about their jealousy.

---

4. Helping Them Name the Feeling

Many people do not like to admit they are jealous. They might say they feel "annoyed," "ignored," or "underestimated" instead. If they dance around the word "jealousy," you can gently guide them: "It sounds a bit like you might feel jealous or afraid of losing something. Is that right?" Do not force them to say "I am jealous" if they are not ready, but giving a name to the feeling can help them see it more clearly.

Once jealousy is named, the person may have a mix of relief and embarrassment. If they say, "Yes, I guess I do feel jealous," respond in a calm, supportive tone: "I understand that can be tough. Let's see if we can figure out what is behind it." You are giving them permission to face that feeling without shame, which can be a big relief.

---

5. Exploring the Root Cause

Encourage the person to think about why they might be jealous:

- **Fear of Losing You:**
  They might worry you will drop them for someone else or forget them as you move up in life.
- **Low Self-Esteem or Past Hurt:**
  Maybe they have a history of being left out, cheated on, or overshadowed. This can cause them to expect similar pain now.
- **Stress in Other Areas of Life:**
  Sometimes, if a friend is struggling at home or work, they become more sensitive in their relationships.
- **Competition for Recognition:**
  A coworker might be desperate to prove themselves, so they feel threatened when you shine. A sibling might fear not being seen by parents who praise you a lot.
- **Miscommunication:**
  They might have overheard something that sounded like you were dismissing them or praising someone else at their expense.

By helping them reflect, you allow them to see their jealousy is not random. It might have a backstory. While you are not their therapist, asking gentle questions can help them connect the dots: "Did something happen before that makes you fear losing close friends?" or "Have you been feeling extra pressure at work?" Let them do most of the talking; your role is to listen with empathy.

---

6. Offering Support Without Encouraging Dependence

When trying to help, there is a balance between being supportive and becoming someone's emotional crutch. If a friend or coworker looks to you for constant reassurance, you risk wearing yourself out. Here are ways to be kind yet maintain boundaries:

1. **Provide a Listening Ear in Moderation:**
   It is okay to say, "I can talk for a few minutes now," but if they always want hour-long calls every day, you might gently limit that.
2. **Suggest Self-Help Steps:**
   After hearing them out, ask if they have hobbies, relaxation methods, or personal goals that could reduce their worries.

3. **Encourage Them to Seek Extra Help if Needed:**
   If their jealousy is deep-rooted, you might suggest they talk with a counselor, especially if they struggle with strong fear or anger.
4. **Set Times or Methods of Communication:**
   If a family member calls you late every night in a panic, you can kindly say, "I care about you, but I need rest, too. Could we talk at a set time each week instead of late at night?"

Having these boundaries ensures you do not become overwhelmed by their anxiety. It also gently shows them that they can take steps to handle their own feelings.

---

7. Helping Them Look at Facts vs. Fears

Jealousy thrives on "What if?" questions. Your friend might say, "What if you like that new friend more? What if you think I am boring?" Encourage them to compare these fears with reality:

- **Ask for Concrete Evidence:**
  "Have I said or done anything that suggests I do not value our friendship?"
- **Show Patterns of Your Behavior:**
  If you have always included them in outings or updates, remind them of that: "We have been friends for years, and I always share my news with you."
- **Discuss Alternate Explanations:**
  If they think a coworker is out to steal your attention, consider simpler reasons. Maybe the coworker is just friendly or happens to pass by your desk often.

This gentle fact-checking can ease the person's mind. It reminds them that they might be mixing worries with real events. By focusing on what is true, the fearful side of jealousy often becomes smaller.

---

8. Encouraging Healthier Comparisons

Sometimes, the jealous person is stuck in a cycle of comparing themselves to someone else. If they keep talking about how they are "not as smart," "not as popular," or "not as skilled," help them see the bigger picture:

- **Different Strengths:**
  Remind them that everyone has unique abilities. If they envy a friend's talent for speaking, mention something they do well.
- **Unseen Challenges:**
  The person they envy might have struggles that are not obvious. They may be good at one thing but dealing with issues in another part of life.
- **Self-Set Goals:**
  Encourage them to measure progress against their past self, not someone else. "Are you improving compared to last month or last year?"

This shift from "I must match or beat that person" to "I can grow in my own way" can reduce jealous urges. Applaud even small steps they take to improve themselves, since it fosters a healthier mindset.

---

9. Suggesting Group or Team Activities

If jealousy is causing friction in a circle of friends or a workplace team, group-based tasks can help ease tension. For example:

- **Cooperative Projects:**
  In a work setting, you might propose a project that uses everyone's strengths. The jealous coworker could see that their contribution is important, too.
- **Shared Interests:**
  If a friend is jealous of your new acquaintances, invite them along to do something everyone enjoys. This helps them feel included rather than pushed aside.
- **Family Game Nights:**
  In families, if one sibling feels overshadowed, group games or joint chores might create a sense of unity. Everyone's role is appreciated.

This approach fosters a "we are in this together" vibe. Instead of competing, people see how each person's input matters. It is not a cure-all, but it might spark more goodwill.

10. Reinforcing Their Sense of Worth

Sometimes, a jealous person needs to hear that they are valued. If it is genuine, simple words can help:

- **"I Care About You."**
  This might seem obvious, but if they worry you will replace them, stating that you value their presence can bring relief.
- **"Your Skills Are Really Helpful Here."**
  For a coworker who feels overshadowed, you might highlight their contributions. Make sure it is sincere and specific: "Your attention to detail saved us from a mistake."
- **"I Appreciate Our Time Together."**
  For a friend or family member, let them know you do not take them for granted. If you truly enjoy shared moments, say so.

Be careful not to overdo it or come across as pitying. Keep it honest and balanced. The point is to remind them that they bring something special to your life or the group.

---

11. Handling Tough Reactions

Sometimes, no matter how gently you approach it, the jealous person might react with anger, denial, or more accusations. They might say, "You are the reason I feel this way," or "You do not get me!" Here is how to cope:

- **Stay Calm:**
  Do not yell back. Keep your voice low and your words measured.
- **Reassure Them of Your Intent:**
  "I am not here to argue; I just want to understand and help if I can."
- **Know Your Limits:**
  If the conversation turns aggressive or if they will not listen, you can end it kindly: "I see this is upsetting. Maybe we can talk again later." Protect your own mental state, too.
- **Consider Mediators:**
  If it is a serious conflict (in a family or work setting), a neutral person—like a counselor, manager, or trusted mutual friend—may help calm the discussion.

Not every attempt will succeed right away. The jealous person might need time to process. You can step back without abandoning them, letting them know you are open to talk again when they are ready.

12. Showing Healthy Behaviors Yourself

If you want to guide someone away from jealous thinking, try to avoid fueling it. For instance:

- **Do Not Brag Excessively:**
  It is fine to share good news, but do so in a friendly way rather than showing off.
- **Include Them When Possible:**
  If the jealous person fears being left out, small gestures like a group invite can ease that fear.
- **Be Fair in Giving Credit:**
  At work, mention teammates' help. At home, thank a sibling for their part in a shared task. This reduces feelings that one person is always in the spotlight.
- **Limit Any Behavior That Feeds Suspicion:**
  If you suspect a friend thinks you are secretly talking behind their back, be careful with private jokes or hush-hush chats that might look suspicious. You do not have to walk on eggshells, but be aware.

Modeling honesty, kindness, and recognition can show them a different way. If they see you treat others in a balanced, open manner, they might feel less threatened.

13. Inviting Them to Shared Problem-Solving

If jealousy is hurting your relationship, treat it as a mutual issue to tackle rather than something that is all on them. Use language like, "How can we both make sure our bond feels safe?" This frames it as a partnership:

- **Plan Activities Together:**
  You could say, "Maybe we can pick a weekly time to hang out so we stay connected."

- **Agree on Communication Boundaries:**
  If a coworker texts you about work matters late at night because they feel insecure, you might compromise on certain times to talk about tasks.
- **Brainstorm Solutions:**
  "If you feel left out when I go to these events, how can we fix that? Would you like to come? Or should I call you afterward to fill you in?"

By turning the problem into a "we" effort, you reduce blame and show you are invested in finding an answer that helps both of you.

---

14. Encouraging Professional Advice if Needed

Sometimes jealousy is tangled with deeper issues—like childhood trauma, severe self-esteem problems, or repeated betrayals in past relationships. In those cases, a friend or coworker might benefit from talking to a counselor or mental health professional. You might gently suggest, "It might be helpful to talk this through with someone who is trained to help people handle strong emotions."

- **Offer Resources:**
  If they seem open, you could share the names of some counseling centers or phone hotlines.
- **Normalize Therapy or Support Groups:**
  Say, "Many people find it useful to get outside perspective."
- **Avoid Pressure:**
  If they resist the idea, do not insist. They might need more time to accept that it can help.

Let them know you still care whether they go to therapy or not, but you believe it could be a positive step, especially if jealousy is leading to constant stress or arguments.

---

15. Watching Out for Signs of Harmful Behavior

A jealous person might cross lines into harmful territory. For instance:

- **Trying to Control Others:**
  They might insist on tracking your every move or telling you whom you can see.

- **Emotional Abuse:**
  They might use guilt, shame, or threats to keep you close.
- **Stalking or Harassment:**
  In extreme cases, jealous individuals might follow you around or send aggressive messages if they fear losing you.

If you suspect the situation is turning unsafe, you need to protect yourself. This could include calling a helpline, talking to a supervisor at work, or involving the authorities if there is any threat. You can still care about them but must not ignore your own safety or well-being.

---

16. Encouraging Them to Find Joy Outside the Relationship

Sometimes, jealousy flares because the person has placed all their sense of self in one bond—whether with you, another friend, or a partner. Gently encourage them to explore hobbies or interests that are separate. You might say:

- "You have always been good with music. Have you thought about joining a local group?"
- "That art project you mentioned sounded fun. Maybe focusing on that would help you relax."

Giving them ideas for personal growth can shift their focus from the fear of being overshadowed to the excitement of their own life. It also reminds them they are not defined only by your friendship or partnership.

---

17. Keeping Your Own Boundaries Strong

Being supportive does not mean letting someone's jealousy dominate your life. You should not have to constantly soothe them or give up your own friendships or goals. Keep an eye on signs that the situation is draining you:

- **Do You Feel Stressed All the Time?**
  If every interaction turns into you reassuring them, you might need to say, "I cannot talk about this again right now."

- **Are You Avoiding Other Activities to Pacify Them?**
  That might mean they are controlling your actions through their jealousy.
- **Do You Feel Guilty Enjoying Your Achievements?**
  A friend's jealousy can make you feel bad about sharing good news, but that is not healthy.

Gently but firmly restate your own needs: "I care about you, but I also need time for my own hobbies and other friends." This is not selfish; it is fair to both of you.

---

18. Checking In After the Storm

Even if you have one good talk and the person seems calmer, jealous feelings can reappear. Make a habit of checking in:

- **Ask, "How Are You Feeling Lately?"**
  Show you remember their worries, but also notice improvements if they have them.
- **Praise Their Effort:**
  If they handled a tricky moment well, say, "I saw you kept cool and did not jump to conclusions. That was great."
- **Stay Tuned for Tension:**
  If events arise that might spark jealousy—like a new project at work or a social event—mention it early and discuss any concerns.

This ongoing care lets them know they are not alone, and it reminds them of the tools they can use to handle jealousy.

---

19. Special Cases: Helping a Sibling with Jealousy

Sibling jealousy can run deep. A brother or sister might feel overshadowed by your achievements or worry about losing parental attention. To help:

1. **Offer Teamwork:**
   Suggest working together on a task or game so they can see you are partners, not rivals.

2. **Share Resources:**
   If you have knowledge or experience, teach them. Show that their success does not threaten you.
3. **Highlight Their Strengths:**
   Let them hear that you admire them for something—sports, humor, creativity. Being noticed can reduce jealousy.
4. **Encourage Family Talks:**
   If parents often compare siblings, you can gently request fairness. "Can we talk about each of our strengths rather than putting us side by side?"

Remember, you cannot fix all family patterns alone. But being a warm presence can help ease sibling rivalry.

---

20. Accepting Your Limits and Letting Go of Guilt

You might do everything you can—listening, guiding, encouraging—but the jealous person still struggles. It is not your job to heal them fully, and you should not feel guilty if they choose not to change. Jealousy can be deeply rooted, and sometimes it takes professional intervention or a big shift in their personal life for them to manage it better.

If they continue to act in ways that hurt you or do not respect your boundaries, you might have to step back from the relationship. This is sad, but your own mental health is important. You can let them know you still care but need some distance until they are ready to handle jealousy in a healthier way. That is not abandonment; it is self-care.

Conclusion

Helping someone handle jealousy is a delicate process. You need empathy, patience, and good boundaries. By seeing the signs early and offering a listening ear, you can invite them to open up about the root cause of their fears. You can remind them of facts that challenge their jealous thoughts, encourage them to focus on their own growth, and show them you value the bond.

But remember, you cannot solve jealousy for another person. They must be willing to face their own emotions and make changes. You can point them toward healthier habits, mention the idea of counseling if needed, and provide emotional support. At the same time, be sure to protect your own well-being so you do not get pulled into a cycle of constant reassurance.

In the best cases, your understanding and gentle suggestions can steer a friend, sibling, or coworker away from the worst parts of jealousy. This can lead to a stronger, more trusting bond. In other instances, your help might at least reduce some of the tension, even if the person's jealousy does not vanish altogether. Either way, offering kindness and honesty can go a long way toward easing the fears that feed jealousy—and possibly sparing your relationship from bigger damage in the future.

Chapter 18: Jealousy in History

When we talk about jealousy, we often think about our own lives—friends, family, love, or work. Yet, jealousy is not new. It has been around as long as people have cared about status, belongings, or relationships. Throughout history, this powerful feeling has driven stories, shaped myths, and even sparked conflicts on a grand scale. In this chapter, we will take a look at how jealousy has appeared in different eras and cultures. We will see how it shows up in myths, how it influenced major events, and how thinkers tried to explain or manage it. By viewing jealousy through a historical lens, we can better understand its strong hold on human hearts and why it remains such a core emotion today.

---

1. Ancient Myths and Legends

From the earliest recorded stories, jealousy has been a key theme. In many myths, gods and goddesses fight or plot because they fear losing worshipers, power, or love.

1. **Greek Mythology:**
   The Greek gods often competed for praise. Hera, wife of Zeus, was famously jealous of his many affairs. Her jealousy led her to punish Zeus's lovers or their children (such as Hercules). This portrayed jealousy as fierce and destructive, yet also somewhat understandable, given Zeus's actions.
2. **Egyptian Stories:**
   In some tales, gods battled over who would be the main deity or who was favored by the people. The god Seth was jealous of his brother Osiris's popularity, which led to major strife, including Osiris's death and a lengthy cycle of revenge.
3. **Norse Legends:**
   Loki, known for trickery, sometimes stirred up jealousy among the gods to cause chaos. Rivalries over magical items or attention from higher powers often fueled these legends, showing how envy and jealousy might unravel even mighty beings.

In these myths, jealousy is not just a passing feeling. It is a force that changes destinies. By reading these stories, ancient people learned cautionary lessons: be wary of letting envy or romantic jealousy grow too big, or you could set off a chain of tragic events.

2. Jealousy Among Rulers and Kingdoms

As civilizations grew, jealousy moved from myths to real-life courts and palaces. Kings, queens, and emperors often worried about losing land, wealth, or loyalty. This kind of jealousy involved protecting a throne, an alliance, or a dynasty.

1. **Pharaohs and Court Politics (Ancient Egypt):**
   Pharaohs needed to secure loyalty from their courts. If a high official seemed too popular, the ruler might suspect them of wanting power. This suspicion, rooted in jealousy or fear, could lead to the official's downfall. Rival queens or consorts might also stir drama if they feared losing the pharaoh's favor.
2. **Imperial China:**
   Emperors had many concubines, and jealousy within the palace could be lethal. Some historical notes mention concubines plotting against each other, using small conspiracies to ensure their children would be heirs. If the emperor favored one woman too much, others felt threatened.
3. **Medieval Europe:**
   Royal courts were full of knights, nobles, and advisors. A king might be jealous of a lord who held too much sway, worrying about betrayal. Noble families competed for land or marriage ties. We see accounts of secret deals and betrayals fueled by envy—someone might want a bigger realm, a marriage link, or to outrank a rival.

In all these settings, jealousy could push rulers or nobles to exile rivals, start wars, or arrange strategic marriages. The price was sometimes high, with entire kingdoms torn apart by jealous ambitions.

3. Jealousy in Great Epics and Literature

From plays to poems, writers have woven jealousy into their plots to captivate audiences. Some of the most famous works revolve around characters driven by envy or fear of being replaced.

1. **Shakespeare's Plays:**
    - **Othello**: Arguably the most well-known story of jealousy, with Iago planting seeds of doubt about Othello's wife, Desdemona. Othello's jealous rage leads to tragedy.
    - **The Winter's Tale**: King Leontes wrongly suspects his wife of being unfaithful with his friend, causing heartbreak and loss for many years.
2. **Alexandre Dumas and The Three Musketeers:**
   Court intrigues in 17th-century France often revolve around jealous plots. Characters fear losing a royal's trust or a lover's attention, which sparks duels and secret missions.
3. **Dostoevsky's Novels (19th-century Russia):**
   Though not always the main theme, envy and jealousy color the conflicts among characters who fight over money, status, or love. These books show jealousy's effect on the mind—how it can make a person both cunning and self-destructive.

Through these stories, readers saw jealousy's consequences: it could turn loving hearts cruel and wise minds blind with doubt. Writers used it to explore human nature, reminding us that envy can corrode even the strongest relationships if left unchecked.

---

4. Historical Conflicts Driven by Jealousy

Some real-world conflicts, big or small, had jealousy as a hidden spark. Leaders or entire groups might resent neighbors who seemed richer or more advanced.

1. **City-State Rivalries (Ancient Greece):**
   Athens and Sparta had different forms of government and cultures. Some historians suggest that envy of Athens's wealth, power, and alliances fueled Sparta's hostility, leading to the Peloponnesian War—a conflict that lasted decades.
2. **Colonial Ambitions:**
   European powers in the 15th to 19th centuries raced to claim lands overseas. Although greed, trade, and resources were major factors, envy also played a role. If one nation saw another gaining riches in the New

World, it wanted the same. Jealous competition spurred more voyages and sometimes violent takeovers.
3. **Regional Hostilities:**
In many parts of the world, a neighboring country's success might lead another to feel overshadowed, sparking wars or attempts to topple the other's monarchy. For instance, the Hundred Years' War between England and France (14th–15th centuries) was fueled by dynastic claims and envy of territory and influence.

While not every conflict can be blamed entirely on jealousy, historians note that envy or fear of losing status often added fuel to existing tensions.

---

5. Religious and Philosophical Views on Jealousy

Throughout history, religious and philosophical teachings tried to guide people away from harmful envy and jealousy.

1. **Biblical Teachings:**
Stories like Cain and Abel show how jealousy between siblings led to the first murder, highlighting its destructive force. Many passages in the Bible warn believers to avoid envy and be content with what they have.
2. **Buddhist Thoughts:**
Buddhism encourages letting go of attachments and comparisons. Wanting what others have or fearing loss is seen as a root of suffering. Mindfulness is taught as a path to see beyond envy.
3. **Islamic Teachings:**
The Quran and Hadith often mention humility and gratitude as ways to avoid envy. Believers are encouraged to trust in divine wisdom rather than compare themselves too much.
4. **Ancient Greek Philosophers:**
Aristotle wrote about envy as pain at the sight of others' good fortune. The Stoics urged control of emotions so one would not be ruled by envy or jealousy.

These spiritual and philosophical paths agreed that jealousy disrupts peace of mind. They often advised gratitude, self-reflection, or trust in a higher plan to counter feelings of envy.

6. Jealousy as a Tool of Politics

Some rulers or political figures used jealousy to manipulate crowds or rivals. They might play groups against each other, stoking envy so that the groups would fight rather than unite.

1. **Divide and Rule Strategies:**
   The Roman Empire sometimes maintained control over conquered lands by favoring one local tribe or leader. This made others jealous and less likely to join forces against Rome.
2. **Feudal Lords:**
   A medieval lord might give small favors to some knights or vassals but not others, hoping the jealous competition would keep them too busy arguing to challenge his power.
3. **Modern Politics in Some Cases:**
   Even in more recent centuries, leaders have been known to highlight differences—stirring envy or resentment among social classes—to draw attention away from their own issues.

Such uses of jealousy show that it can be a potent weapon in the hands of those who know how to provoke emotional reactions among groups.

---

7. Romantic Jealousy Across Time

Jealousy in love stories is not a modern invention. Many famous affairs and romantic dramas in history stemmed from fear of losing someone's affection.

1. **Medieval Courtly Love:**
   Knights would vow loyalty to a noble lady. If the lady smiled upon another knight, jealousy might erupt in duels. Ballads sang of heartbreak caused by unfaithful lovers.
2. **Royal Arranged Marriages:**
   Monarchs often married for alliances, not love. If a king or queen found real affection outside the marriage, it could cause jealousy among the court or even spark rumors of treason.
3. **Scandals in 18th- and 19th-Century Europe:**
   Aristocrats sometimes had open "friendships" beyond marriage. Jealous spats led to famous duels or divorces that scandalized society pages.

We see that while traditions and social rules changed, the basic feeling remained the same: a fear that the beloved would turn their attention or devotion elsewhere, leading to heartbreak or social disgrace.

8. Artistic Depictions of Jealousy

Painters, sculptors, and musicians have long tried to capture the intensity of envy or jealous dread.

- **Classical Paintings:**
  Works might show mythological scenes of jealous gods or a ruler's suspicious glare. Artistic elements—dark clouds, stormy seas—were used to symbolize the turmoil of jealousy.
- **Operas and Ballets:**
  Many famous operas revolve around characters plotting due to jealousy. For example, in "Carmen" by Bizet, jealousy plays a key role in the tragic ending. In Tchaikovsky's ballet "Swan Lake," the sorcerer's trick to confuse the prince with an identical lookalike of the heroine also has notes of jealousy and deception.
- **Romantic-Era Literature:**
  Writers took envy and jealousy to dramatic heights, describing them as storms in the heart. Themes of unrequited love or betrayal soared in popularity, showing how jealousy can drive people to extremes.

These artistic works resonate because the audience can feel the raw power of jealousy, even if they have never experienced it to such dramatic lengths. Art remains a mirror that shows us the intensity of our own emotional possibilities.

9. Attempts to Control or Punish Jealousy

Throughout history, people realized that uncontrolled jealousy could tear communities apart. Some societies tried to handle it with rules or moral teachings.

1. **Adultery Laws:**
   In various cultures, harsh laws against adultery aimed to stop jealous rage

or social unrest. However, these laws could also be misused, with innocent people sometimes punished due to false accusations by a jealous spouse.
2. **Honor Codes:**
In certain places, if a person felt jealous due to a partner's supposed wrongdoing, they might challenge the rival to a duel. This was seen as a way to "defend one's honor." The result was often violence or death, showing how strongly jealousy could fuel dangerous acts.
3. **Councils or Courts Handling Disputes:**
In medieval Europe, local courts sometimes dealt with jealousy-driven conflicts. People might come before a council to complain a neighbor was lying or stealing out of envy. Settling these arguments was important for social peace.

These measures show that societies recognized jealousy as more than a minor emotion; it was a force that could disrupt families and entire communities if not addressed.

10. Changes Over Time: From Secret to Open Discussion

In earlier periods, jealousy might have been seen as something shameful or as an unchangeable flaw. People might keep it hidden or express it through covert means. Over the centuries, however, the idea of discussing emotions openly gained traction, especially in some modern cultures. Now:

- **Psychology Emerged as a Field:**
  In the 19th and 20th centuries, psychologists like Sigmund Freud examined how envy shapes relationships. Later thinkers built on these ideas, helping people see jealousy as a feeling that can be understood and managed.
- **Advice Columns and Self-Help Books:**
  In the 20th century, newspapers and magazines often had "agony aunts" offering tips on relationship problems, including jealousy. This made the topic less hidden.
- **Modern Relationship Counseling:**
  Couples therapy and group therapy sometimes center on jealousy issues. People are encouraged to talk things through rather than hide them.

Thus, while jealousy remains powerful, many modern approaches say open communication and self-examination can keep it under control—lessening the need for drastic actions we read about in older times.

---

11. Famous Historical Figures and Their Jealousy

Some well-known leaders or icons had public struggles with jealousy:

1. **Napoleon Bonaparte:**
   The French emperor was reportedly jealous of his wife Josephine's past suitors. Despite his grand achievements, he felt uneasy about her loyalties.
2. **Henry VIII of England:**
   His six marriages are legendary. Some historians note that jealousy of potential rivals or desire for a male heir made him quick to accuse his wives of unfaithfulness.
3. **Catherine the Great (Russia):**
   Though a strong ruler, some accounts suggest she feared betrayal among her court. While not always pure jealousy, her watchful eye might have been partly rooted in not wanting to lose power.

Their stories illustrate that no matter how grand or powerful a person is, the fear of loss or betrayal can still stir fierce jealousy.

---

12. Lessons History Teaches Us About Jealousy

When we reflect on these tales—myths, royal feuds, wars, or personal dramas—a few lessons shine through:

1. **Jealousy Is Universal:**
   It appears in every culture, every class of society, and every era. There is no group completely free of its reach.
2. **It Can Shift the Course of Events:**
   From small village disputes to entire wars, jealousy can tilt the balance, sometimes with huge consequences.

3. **Open Talk Helps, While Secrecy Fuels It:**
   History shows that hidden jealousies led to plots, poisonings, or betrayals. By contrast, many philosophical or religious traditions promoted open confession or reflection to curb envy's power.
4. **We Are Still Vulnerable:**
   Even though we know these stories, modern people can still fall into jealous traps. The difference is we now have more tools—therapy, open dialogue, and scientific understanding—to address it.

---

13. The Ongoing Impact of Past Stories

Historical episodes of jealousy still shape how we think today. We see them in:

- **Popular Movies and Series:**
  Period dramas often show royal courts swirling with envy and hidden motives, reminding us how emotions can sway big decisions.
- **Language and Idioms:**
  Phrases like "green with envy" can trace back to older references (some credit Shakespeare for popularizing the idea of green as the color of envy).
- **Cultural Attitudes:**
  Some societies remain cautious of "showing off" success for fear of arousing envy in neighbors—an attitude formed by centuries of seeing how envy can lead to conflict.

---

14. Modern Perspectives on Historical Jealousy

Historians and anthropologists study old stories of jealousy to see how relationships, power structures, and social norms developed. They notice patterns, such as:

- **Economic Factors:**
  When resources are scarce, envy tends to rise, leading to more jealousy-fueled disputes.
- **Moral and Ethical Frameworks:**
  Societies with strong moral codes around humility or sharing might reduce jealousy-driven behavior.

- **Social Class Systems:**
  Rigid hierarchies, where people cannot easily move up or down, can deepen feelings of envy, as those in lower ranks see no hope of rising.

These studies help us learn that jealousy is not just personal but also shaped by the environment we live in. If a community values fairness and open communication, jealousy might be less explosive.

---

15. Comparing Past and Present Attitudes

In many ways, humans have not changed. We still care about love, recognition, and status. Yet the way we deal with jealousy is different:

1. **Greater Emotional Awareness:**
   We have fields like psychology, counseling, and therapy. People are encouraged to talk about their feelings rather than hide them.
2. **Less Tolerance for Extreme Acts:**
   In many places, duels or "honor killings" are illegal. Society now sees them as cruel or barbaric.
3. **Accessible Information:**
   People can read articles or watch videos on handling jealousy. Advice is widely shared, not locked away in the palaces of the elite.
4. **Social Media Challenges:**
   On the other hand, the modern world has new triggers for envy—seeing curated images of others' perfect lives can spark jealous thoughts, but that is a new angle.

So while we do not usually fight sword duels over jealousy, we might face a flood of social media comparisons. Each era has its own forms of this ancient emotion.

---

16. Reflections on Past Attempts to "Stamp Out" Jealousy

History contains examples of communities trying to remove envy entirely. Some religious orders or utopian movements preached shared ownership of goods so no one would feel envious. Yet total removal often did not work. People might still compare who does more chores or who is favored by the leader. This suggests that jealousy is deeply human, not erased by rules alone.

At the same time, some cultural norms—like praising collective success or teaching children from a young age to share—helped reduce jealous behavior. Communities that built traditions of cooperation found ways to keep envy from boiling over, though it never disappeared fully.

---

17. How History Shapes Our Future

Looking back shows that jealousy can start wars, ruin friendships, or inspire great stories. But it can also be managed with thoughtful systems—like fair laws, open communication, and personal reflection. As we move forward:

- **We Can Learn from Mistakes:**
  Seeing how envy led to destructive wars or broken alliances might urge modern leaders to seek more diplomatic, transparent methods.
- **We Can Value Education:**
  Teaching people from early on to handle emotions can reduce fear-based decisions.
- **We Can Promote Honest Dialogue:**
  The difference between a tragic outcome and a peaceful solution often lies in talking openly before jealousy grows too big.

The more we understand the past, the more we see patterns in how envy flares and how it can be resolved. This helps shape better policies, better relationships, and a better grasp on our own emotional realities.

---

18. Continuing the Thread: Jealousy's Ongoing Presence

Jealousy endures in modern life, but it is not always about thrones or territory. It might be about who gets the promotion or who has the bigger online following. The human heart still grapples with comparisons, pride, and fear of losing what it holds dear. In the future, we may face new triggers—from advanced technology to rapidly changing social norms. Yet the lessons from history remain useful:

1. **Honesty and Fairness Matter:**
   Where systems are transparent and just, envy has less room to grow.
2. **Understanding Human Nature:**
   People often want to feel seen and valued. If that is lacking, jealousy may rear its head.
3. **Managing Emotions Wisely:**
   Cultures that encourage mindful reflection tend to handle envy better than those pushing it underground.

Conclusion

Jealousy's story stretches back to the earliest myths and continues to shape personal and public life today. Rulers fought wars because of it. Artists captured its essence in plays, paintings, and songs. Philosophers and religious leaders taught ways to rise above it, while entire societies sometimes got swept away by its force. Through it all, jealousy has remained a normal yet risky emotion—a sign of what we hold close and fear to lose.

Examining these historical threads reveals timeless truths: jealousy can spark creativity or destruction, can lead to personal growth or bitter tragedy. It has been both a source of cautionary tales and a driver of great drama. In our own lives, we can learn from these wide-ranging examples. By speaking openly, making fair rules, and understanding jealousy's roots, we steer clear of the worst outcomes seen in ages past.

History reminds us that though jealousy cannot be fully wiped out, we can manage it better with awareness, empathy, and honest effort. The lessons left behind by gods and kings, poets and philosophers, remain relevant. They show how crucial it is to face jealousy without letting it rule us, to respect each other's value while trusting our own. In doing so, we continue writing the long human story of grappling with a feeling that is as old as our desire to hold on to what we love.

Chapter 19: Wrong Ideas About Jealousy

Many people have ideas about jealousy that might not be correct. These ideas can confuse us when we are trying to understand our own feelings or help someone else handle theirs. In this chapter, we look at some common beliefs about jealousy and check if they are true. By clearing up these misunderstandings, we can become better at spotting and dealing with real jealous thoughts. We will use clear examples and keep our explanations simple, without repeating advice or lessons from earlier chapters.

---

1. "Jealousy Is Always a Sign of Strong Love"

A popular myth is that if you really care about someone, you must feel jealous when others come close to them. Some folks even think that if jealousy is missing, it means the bond is weak. However, love does not need constant worry about being replaced. You can value someone while trusting they will remain loyal. Real closeness often grows from respect, kindness, and honest talk, not from suspicion or fear.

In many cases, jealousy can turn love sour. When a person believes it proves "true love," they might excuse actions like checking messages, insulting another person, or giving orders on what a partner can do. This can harm a relationship. Good bonds can include moments of small jealousy, but it is not a must-have sign that the love is real. In truth, calm care and trust often speak more loudly about a strong bond.

---

2. "Jealousy Only Happens in Romance"

Another incorrect idea is that jealousy appears only between people who are dating or married. But jealousy can show up in friendships, at work, in families, or in social groups. A student might feel jealous if a classmate gets more praise from a teacher. A sibling might feel jealous if they think a parent favors another child. A coworker might feel envious if a team member is chosen for a perk.

Focusing just on romantic jealousy overlooks how often people feel threatened outside of love relationships. You can also see it pop up when a friend finds a new friend, or when a family member thinks a parent gives too much attention to a grandchild, leaving others out. Understanding that jealousy is not limited to dating or marriage helps us keep an eye on other corners of life where it might hurt our bonds.

---

3. "Feeling Jealous Means I Am Insecure and Weak"

Some people think that if they are jealous, it means they lack self-confidence or that they are "too fragile." While jealousy might come from low self-esteem at times, it is not always that simple. A person with strong self-confidence can still get jealous if a situation leads them to fear losing something valuable. Maybe they have a solid sense of who they are, but unexpected changes, like a shift in a best friend's behavior, spark that uneasy feeling.

Jealousy can be felt by almost anyone, no matter how confident they normally are. It often ties to how important a certain relationship or status is, rather than only reflecting a person's overall self-belief. Thinking of jealousy as a weakness might keep people from acknowledging it. They might hide their feelings or feel too ashamed to talk them over. This can let the jealousy grow bigger in silence. Realizing that jealousy is not proof of weakness can help people face it honestly.

---

4. "Jealousy Comes from Guilt"

Sometimes, we hear that if you are jealous, it is because you are doing something wrong yourself. For instance, a partner might suspect that you want to cheat on them if they, in fact, are the ones hiding something. While it is true that people with secrets might project their guilt and become jealous, this does not happen every time. Someone can feel jealous due to normal fears or memories of being hurt before. It does not always mean they are guilty themselves.

Blaming jealousy on hidden wrongdoing can damage trust. A person who truly is not hiding anything might feel accused of being dishonest, which can lead to arguments. It is best to consider each situation on its own. Maybe the jealousy appears because someone truly has a history of dishonesty, or maybe it is because the jealous person has old scars. Jumping to the idea that all jealousy comes from secret guilt can stop us from seeing real reasons behind the feeling.

5. "If I Am Jealous, That Means Something Bad Is Definitely Going On"

Some people believe that jealousy is always correct, like an alarm system that never fails. They think, "If I am jealous, it means I must have a reason." While jealousy can happen when there is a real issue (like someone betraying your trust), it can also arise from overthinking or past hurts. The mind can sometimes see threats where none exist.

When a person never questions their jealous thoughts, they might accuse a friend, coworker, or partner unfairly. This can ruin the bond, just because the jealous person did not check the facts. While it is wise to pay attention to signals that something might be off, it is also important to see if the proof matches your fear. Sometimes, jealous feelings come from daydreams or assumptions rather than real events.

6. "Jealousy Keeps Relationships Strong"

Some people say that a pinch of jealousy can act like a spark in a relationship. They argue that it reminds each partner not to take the other for granted. However, jealousy can quickly get out of hand. What starts as a small nudge can become a bigger problem if it leads to control, suspicion, or fights. Rather than making a bond stronger, it might strain it.

Healthy relationships rarely need jealousy to keep partners close. Instead, partners can show care by sharing support, being open about their thoughts, or simply spending meaningful time together. Using jealousy as a trick to keep someone's attention can backfire. The partner might feel manipulated or annoyed. In the end, trust and kindness are safer ways to keep relationships healthy than relying on jealous worries to hold a bond together.

7. "Only Women (or Only Men) Get Jealous"

There is a stereotype that jealousy is more common in certain genders. Some might say women get jealous more often about emotional connections, while men get jealous more about physical or status threats. Others might claim men are more jealous by nature, or that jealousy is a woman's feeling. In reality, jealousy does not care about gender. Anyone can feel it, no matter who they are.

What can differ are the ways people show jealousy, shaped by upbringing or societal norms. For example, if a culture teaches men to hide sadness, men might show jealousy as anger rather than tears. If a culture allows women to express insecurities, they might be more open about jealous thoughts. But these differences do not mean one group experiences more or less jealousy deep down. Viewing jealousy as a "male" or "female" trait is too simple and can keep us from seeing how each person's background plays a role.

---

8. "You Must Hide Jealousy or It Will Ruin Everything"

Some people think jealousy should never be talked about. They believe discussing it will blow it out of proportion and destroy trust. However, hiding jealousy often creates bigger problems. The feeling might grow in secret, leading to silent anger, secret revenge, or sudden outbursts. Openness, handled gently, can relieve tension.

It is true that screaming or accusing someone out of jealousy can push them away. But calmly explaining, "I have been feeling a bit uneasy about how things have changed between us," can open a door to fix the root of the worry. By talking it out in a measured way, we give jealousy less power. The person hearing it can clear up misunderstandings or help find a solution, rather than the feeling building up unspoken until it erupts in a harmful way.

---

9. "Jealousy Only Happens to People with Low Morals"

Sometimes, we might judge a jealous person as "bad" or "immoral," as if being jealous makes them less deserving of respect. This idea can be damaging. Jealousy is not a sign that someone is morally lacking; it is just a normal emotion that can get strong when we feel threatened. Even kind, honest people can feel it if they sense they might lose a precious bond or opportunity.

Confusing jealousy with moral failure can lead us to shame others instead of understanding them. A coworker who is jealous of a new hire might actually be worried about job security, not harboring a mean spirit. A sibling might show jealousy because they need comfort. Labeling them as "bad" or "sinful" might close off the chance to help them or learn from the conflict. It is better to handle jealousy with empathy, so we can find the real source of the fear.

---

10. "Children Do Not Really Get Jealous"

Another wrong idea is that only teens or adults can grasp the feeling of jealousy. Some assume small children's complaints about sharing toys or attention are just fussiness. But kids can feel jealous strongly, too. A young child might become upset if a parent hugs another sibling or if a friend shares secrets with someone else instead. They might not have the words to say, "I feel jealous," but their actions—crying, pushing, or withdrawing—show it clearly.

Recognizing that children can be jealous helps parents and caregivers respond properly. Ignoring it can make kids think their feelings do not matter. Teaching children how to share, express emotions, and trust that they will still be cared for can reduce jealous reactions. The idea that "They are too young to understand jealousy" misses how important it is to guide them in handling strong emotions early on.

---

11. "To Stop Jealousy, You Must Please the Jealous Person All the Time"

When someone acts jealous, we might think the solution is to give them whatever they want, reassure them constantly, and avoid anything that might set them off. While being kind and helpful is good, bending over backward to please someone's every demand can create new problems. The jealous person might become more controlling, expecting total proof of loyalty at every step.

Instead of meeting every demand, look for healthy communication. Ask, "What specific worry do you have? How can we address it without ignoring each other's freedoms?" Setting limits can help them realize that they must handle their feelings in a balanced way. Fulfilling every jealous request—like reading all your messages or isolating yourself from friends—can harm your own well-being and does not truly solve the root cause of their jealousy.

---

12. "You Can Cure Jealousy Instantly"

Some self-help claims suggest quick fixes: a special trick or phrase to make jealousy disappear right away. But deep emotional patterns rarely vanish with a snap of the fingers. People might learn coping skills or find short-term relief, but lasting change usually requires understanding where the jealousy comes from, building stronger self-belief, and learning better communication.

Believing in instant cures can lead to frustration when the feeling returns. People might think they "failed" because they still get jealous sometimes. But emotions are more layered. A healthier view is to see jealousy as an emotion we can manage and lessen over time, not something we banish at once. Patience and practice often work better than believing in a quick fix.

---

13. "Jealousy Can Be Used to Motivate People"

There is a notion that making someone else jealous will push them to work harder, pay more attention, or try to improve. For example, a boss might praise one employee in front of the rest, hoping the others become jealous and ramp up their efforts. A romantic partner might flirt with someone else to spark jealousy and see if their partner reacts. While this might boost competition briefly, it usually harms trust.

Trying to manipulate feelings by creating jealousy often leads to resentment. The person who feels jealous may respond with anger, fear, or withdrawal. They might put in effort for a little while, but the sense of bitterness can linger. Over time, such tactics eat away at closeness. Real growth in teams or relationships comes from honest feedback, shared goals, and supportive guidance, not from trying to spark jealousy.

14. "All Jealousy Must Be Ended Right Away"

While it is true that intense jealousy can damage bonds, it is also okay to feel small bits of jealousy at times and not panic. The idea that any sign of jealousy must be crushed can create fear of our own emotions. We are human, and sometimes we do not like the feeling that we might lose what we love or need.

Small waves of jealousy can serve as signals that something might need attention—maybe you have not spent enough time with a friend, or you feel uneasy about your place at work. Addressing that signal calmly can lead to a better bond. It is not always about ending jealousy instantly, but rather about using it as a clue that something needs adjusting or a conversation needs to happen.

---

15. "Jealousy Is Always Visible and Dramatic"

We might imagine jealousy as big arguments or stormy behavior. While it can appear like that, it can also be quiet. A person might hide it behind polite smiles, letting it fester. They might act supportive but feel resentful inside. Others might become withdrawn, stepping away from groups because they cannot handle the feeling.

This hidden type of jealousy can be just as damaging. The person might develop secret grudges, sabotage efforts behind the scenes, or talk negatively about someone in private. Quiet jealousy can lead to confusion, because the target might not realize why the relationship feels strained. Noticing subtle hints—like a shift in a coworker's tone or a friend's sudden disinterest—can help us spot hidden jealousy before it grows.

---

16. "Jealousy Is the Same as Envy"

People often use "jealousy" and "envy" as if they mean the same thing. But they can differ in key ways. Jealousy usually involves a fear of losing something (like a friend's attention or a partner's love) to a rival. Envy is more about wanting something that someone else has, such as a new car or a certain talent. While they overlap (you can envy a coworker's skill and also feel jealous if you think you will lose praise), they are not identical.

This distinction matters because how we handle each emotion can differ. If you are envious, you might deal with feelings that you want what someone else has. If you are jealous, you might handle fear that a bond or resource is slipping away. Mixing them up might cause confusion in how we respond. Recognizing the difference helps us choose the right approach.

---

17. "If You Do Not Feel Jealous, You Do Not Care"

Some folks assume that if you never show jealousy, you must not really value the person or thing. This is not true. Caring about someone does not always lead to fearful thoughts that someone else will take them. A confident child can love a parent without worrying they like a sibling more. A stable coworker can enjoy a job without panicking that another employee will steal their role. You can deeply care but trust the situation enough not to dwell on jealous fears.

Sometimes people confuse jealousy with protective concern. You might check on a friend's well-being because you care, but that is not the same as being jealous of someone else's closeness to them. Caring can also show up in cheering them on, celebrating their successes (not using certain banned words but expressing honest happiness), and respecting their independence.

---

18. "Age or Culture Erases Jealousy"

It is also untrue that jealousy only happens in certain ages or cultures. While cultural upbringing may shape how a person shows jealousy, the emotion itself appears worldwide, among both young and old. A senior adult can feel jealous of a younger relative's success, just as a teen might feel jealous of a popular classmate. One culture might encourage open displays of jealousy, another might expect people to hide it, but the feeling can be present in both settings.

Assuming older people or certain cultural groups do not feel jealousy at all ignores human nature. We are social creatures, and as long as we care about relationships, status, or recognition, jealousy can arise. What changes are the ways it is expressed or managed.

19. "Jealousy Is Always Dramatic and Impossible to Control"

Sometimes, we see movies or stories where jealousy leads to grand gestures or huge conflicts. While it can be dramatic, it does not have to be impossible to handle. Many people experience jealousy in smaller, more controlled ways. They might feel a brief pang of worry or a momentary sting, then talk it over or let it pass. Not every jealous thought ends in a loud confrontation.

The idea that jealousy always explodes can scare people into thinking they must push the feeling away or hide it at all costs. But people can learn to handle it by being honest with themselves, talking to someone they trust, or finding healthy outlets for stress. Seeing jealousy as workable (instead of unstoppable) is much closer to reality.

20. "Once Jealous, Always Jealous"

A final myth is that jealousy cannot be changed. Some say, "They have always been the jealous type, and they will never be different." But many people learn new coping skills, seek counseling, or gain insights that help them lessen jealous habits. Growth is possible. We have the capacity to understand why we feel threatened and how we can respond differently.

For instance, someone who was often jealous in their early relationships might become more secure later, once they realize their own strengths and learn better ways to communicate. Or a coworker who used to envy everyone's achievements might find satisfaction in personal goals and become a supportive team member. Seeing jealousy as fixed leaves little room for hope or self-improvement. But seeing it as an emotion we can work on allows us to be kinder to ourselves and others.

Conclusion

Jealousy is an emotion we sometimes misunderstand. Wrong ideas—such as believing it is always good in romance or that it only affects certain groups—can block us from seeing what is really going on. By clearing up these myths, we gain a more accurate view of jealousy's nature. We see that it is common among all kinds of people, can happen in different parts of life, and can be managed with honest communication and self-awareness.

Recognizing these misconceptions also reminds us to avoid shame when jealousy appears. It does not mean we are weak, evil, or doomed. It just signals that something we value feels unsafe. With the right tools and an open mind, we can separate fact from fiction and handle jealousy in a healthier, calmer way. In the next and final chapter, we will look forward to what might happen next with jealousy—how changing times and new research could affect how we see and deal with this strong, ever-present emotion.

Chapter 20: What Might Happen Next with Jealousy

We have explored jealousy from many angles—its origins, its effects on the brain, how it shows up in families, work, and across cultures, as well as ways to handle it. Now, in our closing chapter, we will think about what the future might hold for jealousy. Societies are shifting, and technology is growing fast. New ways of living, working, and relating to one another are emerging. How might these changes affect jealousy? Will people find better ways to keep it at bay, or will modern stress add new forms of jealous worry?

We will examine some trends and possible paths. Of course, nobody can predict the future perfectly, but we can consider how jealousy might show up differently as our world keeps changing. We will keep our ideas fresh, avoiding any repeat lessons we shared in earlier chapters.

---

1. Changing Social Structures

Societies in many parts of the world are moving away from large, tight-knit extended families. More people live alone or in smaller households, and they have broader social circles that stretch beyond hometowns, thanks to travel or the internet. While this can be exciting, it might also mean new reasons for jealousy:

- **Multiple Friendship Groups:**
  A person can have friends from school, work, online gaming, or other parts of life. If they jump between these groups, old friends might worry about being replaced.
- **Fewer Family Ties Nearby:**
  If extended families are scattered, some siblings or cousins might get more direct care from grandparents or parents, leading to jealousy among those who live far away.
- **Community Spaces:**
  As communities form in new ways (co-living setups, digital friend groups), jealousy might shift to concerns like who gets recognized in an online forum or who leads the local group's projects.

At the same time, new forms of trust-building may develop. Maybe smaller households will also mean simpler family jealousy issues. People might find more open relationships among friends or a greater acceptance of each person's diverse circles, leading to less suspicion overall.

---

2. Technology and Jealousy

Technology keeps changing how we connect. Smartphones, social media, video calls, and virtual realities can bring people together across distance, but they also create fresh challenges:

1. **Social Media Comparisons:**
   People already struggle with seeing friends post about successes or special events. This can spark envy or jealousy if someone feels excluded. As social media evolves, new features might reveal even more details about daily life, adding to these worries.
2. **Virtual Reality and Avatars:**
   In the future, many might socialize in virtual spaces, forming online friendships or working relationships with avatars. Jealousy could arise if someone's avatar gets more positive attention, or if a partner bonds with someone in a virtual world.
3. **Artificial Intelligence (AI) Companions:**
   As AI chatbots and digital helpers improve, people might build strong ties with them. Could a person become jealous if their friend or partner prefers talking to an AI companion? Possibly. This scenario might have sounded like science fiction before, but it is now a topic of discussion.
4. **Work from Anywhere:**
   Remote jobs and flexible schedules can help us. But they might also blur lines between personal and professional worlds, leading to new workplace jealousies. A coworker might resent a colleague who seems to do less but still get credit, hidden behind remote setups. Or a manager might show extra kindness to a remote worker, sparking envy in those on-site.

It will be interesting to see if people devise new rules or norms about how to handle the extra flow of personal or work information. If privacy settings improve or we learn to post less about our daily activities, jealousy might be less triggered.

3. Increasing Diversity in Family and Relationship Patterns

Families and close relationships are becoming more varied. Some couples choose not to marry but live together. Some families have two mothers or two fathers, some are blended from past relationships, and others are single-parent homes by choice. Meanwhile, some people practice open or polyamorous relationships. Each arrangement can have its unique jealous tensions:

- **Blended Households:**
  Step-siblings or half-siblings may have different sets of grandparents, leading to jealous feelings about gifts, visits, or attention.
- **Open Relationships:**
  Managing jealousy is a key challenge. Partners might set clear boundaries to handle emotional or physical closeness with others.
- **Chosen Families:**
  People may form "families" with friends rather than blood ties. If one friend feels less included, jealousy might arise in ways we have not fully studied yet.

But with greater openness, some see a chance for better communication skills. People who live in new types of bonds often talk more about boundaries, fairness, and feelings. This might lead to a deeper understanding of jealousy and how to keep it from controlling the group.

---

4. Rise of Personal Development Tools

Over the last few decades, there has been a growing focus on mental health and personal growth. We have many tools—therapies, apps, support groups—that teach emotional management. As these spread worldwide, people might handle jealousy better in the future:

1. **Therapy and Counseling:**
   More accessible mental health services could help folks address jealousy early. Instead of letting it stew, they might learn coping methods such as identifying triggers or using calm words to discuss fears.
2. **Emotional Education in Schools:**
   In some places, children are being taught social and emotional skills at

school. If this trend expands, future generations might know how to spot and handle jealousy from a young age.
3. **Self-Help Apps:**
Mobile tools already exist for stress or mood tracking. Perhaps more apps will appear to help people notice early signs of jealousy. They might log when jealous thoughts pop up and give tips on how to handle them. A quick "check your assumptions" reminder could lower false alarms.
4. **Mindfulness Practices:**
Practices that ground us in the present, like breathing exercises, might become a daily habit for many. This helps keep imaginary jealous worries from running wild. Over time, the idea of pausing and questioning our thoughts might become as common as brushing our teeth.

If these personal development avenues keep growing, jealousy might not vanish, but people could have easier ways to keep it under control. Knowing that helpful support is a tap away might reduce the stigma of admitting to jealous feelings.

---

5. Changing Workplace Cultures

Companies and work communities are learning that a stressed or hostile environment lowers productivity. Jealousy among staff can cause hidden conflicts, sabotage, or poor communication. In the future, more workplaces might adopt clearer policies to curb jealous feelings:

- **Transparent Pay and Promotion Tracks:**
  If employees understand exactly how raises or promotions are decided, there is less room for jealous assumptions.
- **Team-Based Rewards:**
  Instead of praising only the top performer, some firms might reward group achievements, reducing envy over who is singled out.
- **Flexible Roles:**
  If a person can shift to a different role or project without a complicated process, they might feel less stuck and less prone to envy someone else's spot.
- **Mental Health Support in the Office:**
  More places might offer counseling sessions or stress management seminars, guiding employees to talk about tensions before they explode.

As people jump between jobs more frequently, workplaces might also foster an environment of skill-sharing, so employees see each other as collaborators rather than rivals. These changes could reshape how jealousy appears on the job.

---

6. Handling Jealousy in Online Communities

Online forums, gaming groups, or creative hubs can become places of belonging. But they can also see spikes of jealousy if certain members get lots of likes or upvotes. In the future, these platforms might evolve:

- **Algorithms That Promote Fairness:**
  Some platforms may try to make sure content from smaller voices is seen as well, preventing certain members from being the only focus.
- **Community Guidelines Against Manipulative Behavior:**
  If someone stirs jealousy by boasting or undermining others, moderators might step in.
- **Anonymous Features:**
  More spaces may allow members to stay unnamed, removing some of the direct comparisons that fuel envy.
- **Educational Tools for Group Moderators:**
  Volunteers who watch over big groups might learn how to spot jealous disputes early and calm them down with fair rules.

If these measures succeed, online spaces could reduce jealousy-based drama. However, it depends on each platform's willingness to create guidelines that encourage balanced interaction rather than fueling competition.

---

7. Future Research on the Brain

Scientists continue to explore the brain's role in emotions. With better technology—like advanced brain scanning—we might discover more about how jealousy starts and unfolds. This might lead to:

- **Targeted Therapies:**
  If we learn which parts of the brain trigger jealous responses, new methods might help people calm those signals.

- **Personalized Strategies:**
  Some individuals might process emotional threats differently than others. Brain research could guide them to the best coping tools.
- **Earlier Detection of Extreme Jealousy:**
  If brain patterns show signs of dangerously high suspicion or aggression, mental health professionals might intervene sooner.

This area of study is still young, but it offers hope that knowledge of brain mechanics might open doors to more effective ways to handle jealousy.

---

8. Media and Entertainment's Influence

Movies, series, and books often use jealousy to spice up plots. Over time, the way media portrays this emotion can shape our public beliefs. If future media leans toward showing healthier ways of handling jealousy—like open talks or counseling—people might copy those behaviors. On the other hand, if jealousy is presented as "romantic" or "heroic," it might keep wrong ideas alive.

We might see:

- **Shows That Model Good Conflict Solving:**
  Characters may demonstrate calm discussions about fears instead of big blowups.
- **Documentaries on Emotional Skills:**
  More programs might teach viewers about the science behind jealousy, showing real people learning to manage it.
- **User-Created Content:**
  People who overcame jealousy could share their experiences, tips, or interviews, spreading insight to wide audiences.

Media can be a powerful teacher of norms. If it chooses to highlight helpful approaches, future viewers might grow up with a clearer, kinder view of jealousy.

---

9. Global Interactions and Cultural Sharing

As the world connects through travel and digital channels, cultural norms blend. People may adopt elements from other traditions, including ways to handle jealousy. Some cultures historically used group discussions or communal rituals to ease envy. Others taught direct confrontation or strict separation of personal belongings.

In a global environment:

- **Workshops or Seminars:**
  International conferences might host sessions on emotional intelligence, including jealousy management.
- **Shared Online Platforms:**
  People from different regions might swap experiences about how their communities reduce envy.
- **Adoption of Best Practices:**
  If a certain cultural practice—like having a circle talk for emotional issues—proves effective, it may spread to other groups.

Over time, we might see a more blended approach to jealousy, picking from many cultures' strengths.

---

10. AI in Therapy and Coaching

A possible future trend is the growth of AI-based emotional support. We already see some chatbots or phone apps offering basic mental health suggestions. In the future, they could become more advanced:

1. **AI Counselors:**
   People might chat with an AI that can recognize patterns of jealousy in their language. It could then guide them to question their assumptions or practice certain techniques.
2. **Real-Time Advice:**
   Imagine wearing a device that tracks heartbeat or stress signals and alerts you when signs of jealousy spike. The device could offer short instructions, like, "Take three deep breaths and think about the facts of the situation."
3. **Group AI Tools:**
   In workplaces or communities, an AI system might watch interactions for signs of brewing jealousy (tone, repeated friction) and suggest team-building measures before problems get big.

While AI cannot replace genuine human connection, it can help nudge people toward better emotional control. The main question is how comfortable individuals will be with letting technology sense their feelings. Privacy concerns might slow this trend, but the possibility is there.

11. Rising Awareness of Boundaries

The concept of personal boundaries has gained attention in modern times. More people are learning that healthy limits help keep relationships balanced. This might lower jealousy by clarifying who can ask what, who can see certain personal details, and how much time or energy each bond can demand:

- **Clear Social Boundaries:**
  If a friend or colleague knows from the start that you cannot be available 24/7, they might be less likely to become jealous when you spend time elsewhere.
- **Digital Privacy Limits:**
  People may set rules about who sees their photos or personal updates, preventing some forms of social media envy.
- **Consent in Emotional Sharing:**
  Instead of pressuring someone to reveal everything about their contacts or messages, we might respect each other's private spheres. This reduces the breeding ground for jealous snooping.

As boundary awareness grows, individuals might feel more secure, trusting that their relationships are not threatened every time someone else appears in the picture.

12. Possible Shifts in Romantic Expectations

Romantic bonds have changed a lot over the centuries, and they will keep changing. Some see a move toward more fluid relationships, where each partner is honest about their needs and comfortable letting the other have friends of various types. This can lower jealousy if everyone's roles and boundaries are openly agreed upon.

Still, others might cling to old ideals of exclusivity, or they might want a very "traditional" relationship. In such cases, jealousy might remain a key topic if one partner feels the rules are broken. We may see:

- **Flexible Relationship Contracts:**
  Some couples write a list of what is okay and not okay when it comes to friendships, social outings, or online chats. Clear communication from the start helps.
- **Marriage Laws Evolving:**
  In some places, marriage laws or social norms are adapting to new ideas of partnership. More acceptance of varied setups might mean new rules about property, child-rearing, and visiting rights.

How these changes unfold will shape romantic jealousy in the decades ahead.

---

13. Education on Emotions for All Ages

If emotional education becomes standard, it might not stop at schools. Workplaces, community centers, or online courses might teach people from teen years to senior adulthood how to handle jealousy. This could include:

1. **Adult Workshops:**
   Retirees or older adults might learn to handle envy of younger generations' tech skills or life changes.
2. **Family Sessions:**
   Grandparents, parents, and children might sit together, guided by a counselor, to talk about feelings of being left out, sibling rivalry, or changes in attention.
3. **Peer Mentoring Groups:**
   People who overcame strong jealous behaviors might mentor those still struggling, sharing real-world tips.

With widespread access to these resources, jealousy may still appear, but fewer people might see it as a shameful secret. Instead, it could become something we openly address, like stress or anxiety.

14. Reducing Stigma Around Mental Health Support

Stigma about mental health help is dropping in many areas, but not all. If this trend continues, we can expect more people to seek therapy for jealousy issues without shame. They might say, "I am in counseling because I want to feel more secure in my friendships," and that could be seen as normal self-improvement. As we remove shame, we might see:

- **Earlier Intervention:**
  People noticing jealous urges could get help before they escalate into bigger conflicts.
- **Better Trained Therapists:**
  Professionals might refine special programs for jealousy, distinct from programs for anger or sadness.
- **Group Support:**
  Small group sessions could let people compare experiences in a safe place, learning from each other's success stories.

---

15. Environmental Challenges and Shared Goals

The future may hold large-scale problems like climate change, water scarcity, or global health crises. Such events can push communities to bond or can raise tensions. On one side, big challenges might unify people, as everyone sees they need to work together, leaving less room for petty rivalries or jealous comparisons. On the other, shortages of resources might spark envy and fear, leading to conflicts over who gets what.

If cooperation wins out, jealousy might shrink in the face of a bigger mission—protecting the environment or ensuring enough resources for all. If competition flares, jealousy could worsen, with groups fighting over limited supplies. Policy choices and public attitudes will likely shape which way this goes.

16. The Balance Between Individual Success and Collective Well-Being

Modern life often rewards personal achievements—high test scores, big paychecks, fancy job titles. This focus on individual wins can fuel envy or jealousy. Some voices call for more group-oriented thinking, praising cooperation and shared progress. If societies shift to a bigger sense of "us" rather than "me," jealousy might be lessened because success is measured by collective betterment, not just personal gain.

We might see:

- **Community-Focused Schools:**
  Students learn group projects and how to help each other excel, lowering the "I must be the top" mindset.
- **Work Policies That Value Team Outcomes:**
  Rewards are given to entire units for achieving goals, reducing the spotlight on a single star.
- **Social Celebrations for Group Achievements:**
  People might highlight steps taken by a whole neighborhood or city, giving credit to everyone.

Though this shift is not guaranteed, any move toward collective well-being could reduce the pressure to outdo each other, which in turn could keep jealousy more in check.

---

17. Ongoing Philosophical and Spiritual Insights

As humans keep exploring meaning and purpose, spiritual and philosophical thoughts about jealousy may evolve. Some modern thinkers might blend ancient wisdom with new findings, suggesting paths to inner peace that address jealousy. We may see:

- **New Mindfulness Movements:**
  Programs teaching individuals to notice jealous ideas without acting on them, guiding them to calm acceptance.
- **Ethical Debates:**
  Discussions on whether society should structure things so that envy is

minimal—like ensuring basic needs for everyone or limiting extreme wealth gaps that make envy so common.
- **Guided Reflection or Retreats:**
  People who join spiritual retreats might delve into their jealous sides, seeking clarity about why they fear losing status or love.

These approaches suggest that as knowledge grows, so do the ways we can handle strong emotions, including jealousy. Instead of ignoring the feeling or letting it reign, we can find deeper understanding through reflection.

---

18. Personal Choice and Adaptation

In the end, jealousy's future partly depends on each person's choices. Technology, culture, and policies matter, but personal adaptation plays a big role too. As we gain knowledge, we can decide how to respond when that little twist of worry appears. Will we feed it with suspicion or try to soothe it by talking openly?

Each new generation might learn from the last how to keep jealousy from becoming a huge barrier. People might be more open about seeing a counselor, reading about emotional skills, or discussing fears with friends. Or they might rely on brand-new tools that make old jealous patterns less likely to arise. In any case, the emotion itself is unlikely to vanish, but our ways of handling it can keep improving.

---

19. Potential Growth of Compassionate Communities

One hope is that as empathy grows, so does our understanding of jealousy. Compassionate communities—where people help each other's well-being—could see jealousy as a sign that someone feels scared, rather than treating it as shameful. Neighbors or coworkers might gently ask, "Are you feeling uneasy? How can we support you?" instead of letting blame or gossip spread.

Such communities would not label jealous people as villains but would invite them to share their worries in a safe space. This approach might minimize the conflict and mistrust that jealousy can bring. While not every place will become a caring utopia, pockets of this thinking could appear, showing a kinder approach to emotional strife.

---

20. Concluding Hopes and Possibilities

Jealousy has been with us for a long time, and it still stirs strong feelings today. But the future gives us reasons to hope. We have better science, more mental health resources, and broader cultural awareness. We also have challenges—like technology's effect on personal ties or the strain of resource shortages—that might make jealousy show up in new ways.

Overall, we can guide jealousy toward less harmful forms. As more people learn about emotional regulation, open talk, and trust-building, they can catch jealous fears early and handle them with care. Workplaces can replace harsh competition with supportive teamwork. Families can blend old values with modern methods of sharing feelings. Online spaces can adopt fairer systems that reduce envy. And we might even see new breakthroughs in brain research or AI support that help us keep jealousy under control.

Though we cannot know exactly what lies ahead, we can be sure that this emotion will remain part of human life. It signals that we treasure something—love, friendship, status, or security. By facing jealousy head-on, using the insights from science and personal reflection, we can shape a future where jealous thoughts do not lead us into ruin but become a reminder to care for our bonds in healthier ways. We hope this book has given you a clearer sense of jealousy's roots and possibilities, so you can play a role in building more stable, trusting, and understanding relationships, both now and in times to come.

With this, we have reached the final chapter of our look at jealousy: its nature, its myths, its presence in various parts of life, and now its potential future. People will always feel a twinge of fear or envy when they value something and see a threat. But as we learn more about ourselves and each other, we can respond with fairness and compassion. That is the ongoing task—both a challenge and an opportunity—for anyone who seeks to live with fewer worries and stronger ties in a world where jealousy need not rule our hearts.

www.ingramcontent.com/pod-product-compliance
Lightning Source LLC
LaVergne TN
LVHW012104070526
838202LV00056B/5621